What some a
Call Me Blue

When I think of Duane Blue, the word that stands out first and foremost in my heart is the word *grace*. It is nothing short of the amazing, marvelous grace of God that can so radically change a man. It is, indeed, an Apostle Paul-type story of an encounter with a Holy God who makes a hellion into a holy man. Read, be blessed, and pass it on.

—Johnny Hunt, *Senior Pastor*
First Baptist Church,
Woodstock, Georgia

Ron Owens has done it again. After writing superb biographies of two of the most unforgettable people one will ever meet, he has centered this one around the story of Duane Blue. Blue, the name by which his friends know him, was a drug-busting, motorcycling, wasted piece of humanity until Jesus radically changed his life. You will read *Call Me Blue* with great pleasure and gratitude.

—Roy Fish, *Professor* (retired)
Southwestern Baptist Theological Seminary,
Fort Worth, Texas

If you ever want to meet a real, transparent, open and honest believer who loves Jesus and His Word with all his heart, then you need to know Duane Blue, or "Blue," as we call him. The story of how God reached out to his wife Iris, and then through her, touched Blue's life, is just awesome. I'm so grateful to Ron Owens for writing this book.

When I first met Blue it was immediately obvious I'd met a brother, and the refreshing thing about him is that he didn't have any "church baggage" to hold him back. Oh how I love Blue.

One day I gave him a copy of the Hebrew-Greek Study Bible edited by Dr. Spiros Zodhiates, and he proved to me that a believer doesn't have to have a theological education to get into the original language and understand God's Word. Blue proved to me that one only needs to have a hungry, yielded heart, and know that the Holy Spirit is his teacher. Blue literally devoured this study Bible and continues to do so.

It doesn't surprise me that God is using Blue and his wonderful wife, Iris, all over the world because they both have been willing to just be surrendered vessels who simply allow Christ to live His life in and through them.

You will love this book, and it will so excite you to think that there are other "Blues" out there, many who are perhaps living in a bus like he once did, who need to hear about Jesus. We are often guilty of writing these off, not realizing that they too can become surrendered vessels, like Blue, who broke all the molds, and be used of God to touch thousands of lives.

—Wayne Barber, *Senior Pastor*
Woodland Park Baptist Church,
Chattanooga, Tennessee

For more than 25 years I've admired Blue and his sweetheart, Iris. They are *God's Dynamic Duo!!*

Blue is real, genuine, authentic, classic, unique, and hewn out of God's quarry of spiritual characters. Get yourself a cup of Dark Roast with a bowl of cookies—kick back and have the read of a lifetime! Blue's testimony will blow you away. Put on your seatbelt!!

—Dennis Swanberg, *The Man Code*
Monroe, Louisiana

Most individuals standing beside Duane Blue would be dwarfed by his physical size. After reading *Call Me Blue* one feels like a spiritual dwarf in comparison to this giant of faith in action. In this intriguing biography, Ron Owens presents us with the unfolding riches of God's grace in the life of Duane Blue. God delights in displaying His trophies of grace, and Duane and Iris Blue are two of His trophies which He delights in continuing to display to bring Him glory!

—E. A. Johnston, Ph.D., *Author*
Fellow of the Stephen Olford Center for Biblical Preaching,
Memphis, Tennessee

In the book, *Wild Goose Chase,* by Mark Batterson, he writes that the Celtic Christian had a name for the Holy Spirit: *Geash-Glas,* or *Wild Goose.* This hints at the mysterious nature of the Holy Spirit. Like a wild goose, the Spirit of God cannot be tracked or traced.

This is a perfect description of Duane Blue and his journey with Christ. God is the only explanation for his life and ministry. You are about to be challenged in how you live out your faith in Christ. Simply put—trust and obey. That's it! Blue has lived this principal through the years and God continues to use it, day by day, for His glory.

—Jonathan Beasley, *Senior Pastor*
The Church at Arkansas,
Fayetteville, Arkansas

CALL ME
BLUE

How a lying, cheating, stealing, lonely
drug-and-booze addict was transformed
into a New Creation.

RON OWENS
with Duane Blue

CrossHouse Publishing
P. O. Box 461592
Garland, TX 75046-1592
www.crosshousepublishing.org

ISBN: 978-1-61315-007-8
Library of Congress: 2011928515

Table of Contents

Foreword

Ron Owens has written this wonderful book about a man whose life reminds the reader of the life and conversion of Saul, who after his salvation experience wrote,

"Here is a trustworthy saying that deserves full acceptance: Christ Jesus came into the world to save sinners—of whom I am the worst. But for that very reason I was shown mercy so that in me, the worst of sinners, Christ Jesus might display his unlimited patience as an example for those who would believe on him and receive eternal life" (1 Timothy 1:15-16).

From time to time God puts a life on display so that men and women everywhere can see and know that if God would patiently, lovingly draw a man like that into a personal relationship with Himself, then everyone can be assured that God, through Christ, can change their lives as well.

That's the story of my dear friend, Duane Blue. He is a living example, a life on display, of the grace of God that can take the worst of the worst and make him or her a radiant member of the family of God.

I first met Duane Blue through my mentor and friend, Dr. Carlos McLeod, who at that time was Director of Evangelism for the Baptist General Convention of Texas. Duane, or as we affectionately call him, "Blue," had married Iris Urrey and the two of them gave their testimony at the Texas Evangelism Conference. Almost immediately I invited them to speak at the church I was a pastor of at the time—*Southcrest Baptist Church* in Lubbock, Texas. From that point on, our friendship has grown.

I became Associate Director of Evangelism under Dr. McLeod and Iris and Duane began to work as Mission

Service Corps volunteers with the Evangelism Division of that Convention as well as for, what was then, the Home Mission Board of the SBC. Today they continue to work in that same capacity with The Southern Baptists of Texas Convention as well as with the North American Mission Board of the Southern Baptist Convention. As the Director of Evangelism I have the joy of working closely with the Blues.

Ron Owens is an excellent writer whose words give an artist-like description of Blue from his childhood up into his adult years that would cause the average churchgoer to shake his head in disbelief.

As a child, Blue had undiagnosed dyslexia which caused him to struggle in school and to eventually drop out in his early teens. His dad married multiple times and destroyed the life of every woman he was married to. Blue got into dope at 13 and became very rebellious. He developed a lifestyle which led him to a state of deep loneliness and hopelessness. This is a story that most people could not begin to imagine.

Blue's "Damascus Road experience" is one of the most fascinating conversions in the history of the Christian faith. How he met Iris, and how she led him to the Savior while talking to him in a phone booth a thousand miles away, will make you want to shout.

His experiences during the beginning days of his Christian walk will have you laughing until tears flow and weeping at his sincere innocence. This is a "must read" book! Ron Owens writes in such a way as to literally capture your attention and reminds the reader of God's power to change a life, giving it purpose, direction, and hope where there had been nothing but a destructive lifestyle of hopelessness. This is the story of a man who once was looked upon as "the scum of society," who hated everyone including himself. He was captured by the Evil One and could not escape on his own. Then came Jesus who set the captive free!

Today Duane Blue is one of the most transparently real followers of Jesus Christ I personally know. If ever there was a man who personifies 2 Corinthians 5:17 in an indisputable way, it is Blue. *"Therefore, if anyone is in Christ, he is a new creation; the old has gone, the new has come!"* This is a man who lives and speaks about his faith daily. Like Paul, Blue is, *"Not ashamed of the gospel, because it is the power of God for the salvation of everyone who believes"* (Romans 1:16). Blue has never forgotten where God brought him from and where he would have been today apart from Jesus.

This book needs to be put in the hands of the worst of sinners and read by the self-righteous pretender who is blinded by the Evil One. Any honest seeker of truth will find the truth in this book.

This account of my friend will cause the follower of Jesus to humbly return to his "first love." It is my prayer that this record of Blue's life will be placed in the hands of young people, mature adults, unbelievers, as well as followers of Jesus as a witness of God's saving grace found only in the Lord Jesus Christ.

—Don Cass, *Director of Evangelism*
The Southern Baptists of Texas Convention

Acknowledgements

<u>A very special thanks to:</u>

—those who took time out of their busy schedules to read a draft of *Call Me Blue* and write a response.

—the many "friends of Blue" who have contributed testimonies about the impact he has had on their lives over the years.

—those extra sets of ears who not only patiently sat through my reading of the manuscript, but who made valuable suggestions.

—Duane Blue for the privilege of putting the story of his life down on paper.

—my wife, Patricia, who has been my "chief critic, editor, and encourager" throughout this writing project.

—CrossHouse Publishing who is always a joy to work with. It is rewarding to be able to talk person-to-person with a publisher, knowing you are more than just another "project number."

—those who have faithfully prayed for me throughout the writing of this incredible story of God's grace.

And finally, but most importantly, to Blue's God, and ours, who transformed this lying, cheating, stealing, booze and drug addict into a brand new creation in Christ. Only God!

A Word from Blue
The Ingredients of Life

If you're baking a cake or cooking a stew, what you end up with depends upon the ingredients you put in it. It's much the same way with life. That's what it was like for me. For years the ingredients I put in my life, and the choices I made, caused me years of loneliness, loss of family and friends.

In the Garden of Eden, God told Adam that it was not good for him to be alone. And it is the same for all of us. We are not designed to be alone. But it wasn't until I came to know Jesus Christ in March 1984 and joined Central Baptist Church, near where I lived in my bus, that I experienced what it meant to be part of a family. I would never be alone again. I still have great and loving relationships with people from that church who impacted my life and helped me learn to read and write and grow as a Christian. It blows my mind to think that now I even study Greek and Hebrew in my own personal Bible study.

God intended life to go from glory to glory—a life that is richer than anything we possibly could imagine. Nothing this world offers comes anywhere near that, because of the lack of one ingredient: the Lord Jesus Christ. But it's not just believing in Him, it's surrendering to Him in the daily choices we make, adding to our lives the ingredients that please Him, just like the analogy of the cake and beef stew—what you put in them is what you're going to get out of them.

God intends for us to be gemstones in His kingdom, but the greatest gemstone has no value until it is cut and shaped by a master cutter. And that is how it is with our lives. Jesus, the Master Cutter, cuts away the garbage of our past until the true glory of His presence is revealed in our lives. That's when life begins to be something wonderful. It is my prayer that everyone who reads this book will experience what I am saying in their life—the glory of God's presence.

God has given me a wonderful wife, Iris, and through our relationship, an incredible son, Denim. God has so blessed me. It blows my mind that He could take someone as lonely and deep in sin as I was and give me so many wonderful relationships that I now have around the world. These have all come because of the opportunities God has given me to serve him on four continents. In addition to the United States and Canada, I've been to Australia five times; Europe, nine; Israel, 13; and once to Nepal, India and Egypt. And everywhere I've gone I've met new members of "my" family!

Everywhere I go I tell people that I'm married to a beautiful *Ruby* with many facets, that I have a beautifully cut *Diamond* for a son, and that I'm an *Onyx;* but I also tell them that our real value is going to be measured by God one day in eternity. Until then, what we do with our lives in affecting others is going to determine what He's going to say. My prayer is that God will use this book, as well as the book that has been written about Iris' life, to reach someone who is where we used to be, and give them hope that God can give them a new life for the lonely, bitter, foolish life they are now living.

Though there's not time or space to thank everyone who has played a big part in the ingredients that have gone into the "cake" of my life, I'm going to mention just a few. You'll read about some of these in the book.

—**Bobby Conners,** still one of my closest friends, who was the janitor at Central Baptist Church when I got saved and who went on to found, and pastor, New Hope Baptist in Pinehurst, Texas. Though I'm a year older than he is, I still think of Bobby as my father in the Lord.

—**Vlado and Ruth Fajfr** from Czechoslovakia, who impacted Iris' and my life, especially in the area of prayer. They were one of God's greatest blessings to us.

—**Manley Beasley** was like another father to both me and Iris. He opened more doors of ministry for us than anybody else.

—**Johnny Hunt,** pastor of First Baptist, Woodstock, Georgia, who was my pastor and encourager for six of the greatest years of my life.

—**Ron Owens,** the writer of this book, who helped me understand the importance of investing in other people's lives, even when you'd rather have killed them, because, *"where your treasure is, there will your heart be also."*

—**Wayne Barber,** who in 1994 gave me my first *Greek-Hebrew Key Study Bible* and took the time in his office to teach me how to take apart the Word of God to find the deeper meaning in the love letters from our heavenly Father to each of us.

—**Jim Everidge,** who has been my pastor for most of my Christian life, in three different churches. Through all our years of ministry, whenever we've been struggling, we've known we could always ask brother Jim to pray for us. He is one of the most dedicated men of prayer I've ever met.

—And thank you, **Lord Jesus,** for saving a wretch like me, and for allowing me to serve you and to enjoy all the blessings that come from being a part of your family, the family of God!

Finally, I want to thank our new church family, *Sand Springs Baptist Church* in Athens, Texas, and our pastor, Erick Graham, who has a real heart for God. He has asked us to come and help the church in reaching the lost, which is our passion. We believe in the local church. We believe it is God's will for the local church to be His light and salt in this dark world.

We still travel a lot, and we thank God for the doors He continues to open for us to share the gospel, not just in other churches, but in schools, prisons, restaurants, grocery stores, laundromats, elevators, or wherever we have the opportunity to talk about Jesus. We look for all kinds of ways to help others find the one ingredient, the only ingredient, that will change their lives forever. That ingredient is a person. That ingredient is the Lord Jesus Christ.

Introduction

I don't remember if it was actually at the *Prayer and Spiritual Awakening Conference* held at Capital Hill Baptist Church in Washington, DC, in 1985, or somewhere else that I first met Duane Blue. Whether it was in DC or not, I do recall being impacted by the testimony he shared that day. I realized that I was looking at a picture of God's grace with which few of us can identify. There stood this giant of a man, tears streaming down his cheeks, telling us how far God had to stoop to pull him out of his pit of sin.

Looking at the program, I realized that my wife, Patricia, and I were scheduled to follow his testimony with music. What to do? Amazing Grace? That would work. Marvelous Grace? That would fit. As we climbed the steps to the podium, passing Blue who was having a hard time finding the next step through his tears, I whispered to Patricia: *"Chosen."* I thought of 1 Peter 2:9 and looking straight at Blue I sang:

> *You've been **chosen** in Jesus the Savior,*
> ***chosen** to praise His name.*
> ***chosen** to follow His footsteps,*
> *sometimes in suffering and pain.*
> *He who identifies fully with every problem you face,*
> *promises strength in your weakness,*
> *and in each trial His grace!*
>
> ***Chosen, chosen** in Jesus,*
> *learning to be more like Him.*
> ***Chosen** to follow His footsteps,*
> ***chosen** to praise His name.*[1]

---

[1] From the song, *Chosen*. Words by Ron Owens.

By the time I had finished singing the song, you could have picked Blue up with a blotter. It fit his situation so perfectly he thought we had written the song, right on the spot, just for Him. Looking back to that moment, though the song had been written some months earlier, God knew that it was going to be "Blue's song."

Blue is the second longest-serving *Mission Service Corps volunteer* with the North American Mission Board of the Southern Baptist Convention (1985). His wife, Iris, is the longest serving MSCV (1980). At one point, they both were placed under my supervision when I was assistant to Henry Blackaby in the *Office of Prayer and Spiritual Awakening* at that Board. When our paths would occasionally cross I would always find them right in the middle of God's activity, whether witnessing to the lost in every imaginable scenario or sharing the message of revival, calling God's people to return to Him in repentance and surrender.

What I wrote in the Introduction to *Iris: Trophy of Grace,* can be just as well said of this account of Duane Blue's life. *Call Me Blue* is more than history; it addresses many life lessons that are common to us all. In his unique way, Blue provides answers out of his own personal walk with the Lord. The impact he has had on countless lives over the years, whether ministering on his own or with Iris, is affirmed in the tributes and testimonies recorded on these pages.

—**Ron Owens**
March 2011

Section One

A Rough Start

*It is not how well or how badly
you begin that counts; it is
how well you finish.*

1

Dark Days

"I didn't go to her funeral, and I didn't go to her grave. It was almost like I didn't know her, even though she was my mother. I found her dead on the bathroom floor—she had taken over 200 pills, at least that's what the police said. She was 40 years old.

"I don't know what kind of pills they were, but it didn't really matter, I guess. Even the coroner couldn't figure out what all she took so they decided not to call it a suicide. I can't remember what they said it was; all I knew was that she was dead. I felt a bit guilty, but couldn't feel much emotion because we had not really communicated since I had moved to the garage across the street when I was 16. That was five years before.

"My mother was a single parent who worked at the Kalamazoo, Michigan, post office, two blocks away from where we lived. She'd leave at three in the afternoon and return at eleven o'clock each night. She paid the rent on time for her dinky little three-room house—two bedrooms, one bath, and a kitchen connected to a living room full of worn-out furniture. She drove an old car that was always breaking down and she lived as close to nothing as a body could live. I wasn't any help to her; in fact I probably was as much to blame for her suicide as anything because of the life I was living—that and loneliness.

"This time she had succeeded in killing herself. She had tried to do it two weeks before, but a teenager, walking along the alley behind her house, heard a car engine running in the garage. When he saw that the door was closed he knew something was wrong so he opened the garage door and found my mother lying on the floor. She had put a pillow under her head and had covered herself with a blanket. She was still alive.

"They kept her in the hospital for 10 days before deciding that she wasn't really trying to kill herself. They said it was just a cry for help. It was a cry for help alright; the problem was, there was no one to help her. And it sure wasn't going to be me. I was more interested in my next 'high,' which her suicide that afternoon had interrupted."

A bit of Blue history

Blue's mother gave birth to him at St. Luke's Hospital, Denver, Colorado, on March 17, 1951. Two years later they moved to Portage, Michigan, where at the age of six he was "forced" to attend *Portage Central Elementary School*. It was not long before he began to show signs of rebellion, partly because of undiagnosed dyslexia. His teachers didn't know how to handle him, other than a Miss Hall in the 6th grade, who did her best to reach out to him, to "save" him, as she saw Blue becoming more and more rebellious. She knew that he was purposefully getting into trouble so that they would punish him by putting him "in the hall"—exactly what he wanted because he was embarrassed that he couldn't read.

That summer, at the age of 13, Blue began smoking tobacco and marijuana. Also that summer he began showing his creative gifts when, with the help of a few friends, he constructed a seven-room underground hut[2] in the field behind his house where they could retreat to smoke pot without the fear of being caught. It was at this point that they also began to add other drugs to their inventory.

Following that summer of drug adventure, his mother moved to Kalamazoo where Blue entered Loy Norrix High School. He lasted two days before dropping out. He never returned.

---

[2] The building of this underground hut was early evidence of Blue's interest and skills in the field of construction.

Freedom?

"Five years before my mother's death," recalls Blue, "when I moved to the garage across the street, I thought that was going to mean real freedom. I thought I had everything. What more could you ask for? I had my motorcycle, my stereo, my drugs, and I could let my hair and beard grow as long as I wanted. I didn't cut either of them for the next 12 years."

On most afternoons, when his mother left for work, Blue and his pot-smoking, druggie friends turned her house into party-central. They would get high on whatever was available, and would be out of there before she got home. But Blue never "fixed," because he was terrified of needles.

"When I was real small," recalls Blue, "a nurse broke off a needle in my arm giving me a shot. That's why I snorted, that's why I took speed and acid and smoked all kinds of marijuana and hash."[3]

Drugs and jails

Eventually cocaine, marijuana, and alcohol were Blue's top three requirements to make life bearable. Back then his motto was: "Cocaine will get you through times without money, but money will not get you through times without cocaine." So he snorted—a lot of it. To afford his habit, he'd steal bicycles and whatever else he could get away with—but he didn't always get away with it. From ages 13 to 15 he was in and out of jail as a juvenile, usually from 10 to 15 days, then as he got older he would spend up to 30 days behind bars.

Occasionally, however, he would even do some legitimate work. The summer he built the underground drug-hut, he took care of horses and did some haying for a farmer. Not much money, but he did make $3.00 a day, and he got a free meal on top of it.

---

[3] Hash, though processed from the same plant, is a much stronger form of marijuana.

From salesman to thief

Some of us recall hearing the sound of the loud, happy jingle of an ice-cream truck as it drove through our neighborhood. Blue's first real kind of job was running a version of this, from which he sold ice cream bars. He'd get his cart and assigned route in the morning, ring his bell all day, sell the bars, then return to collect 3 cents for every bar he'd sold.

"I made about $9.00 for a full day's work," he recalls. "On a real good day I maybe made $12.00. I thought that was pretty cool. I did that for about a week, until one day, when I was heading back to the store, two guys jumped me and stole all the money I had collected from my sales—$170.00! That's the day I decided to change professions. I decided that it was more lucrative, and took a lot less of my time, to 'rob' ice-cream carts."

That day Blue changed from a salesman to a thief. He figured, why spend a whole day selling when he could beat a guy up and take all the money he had in a few minutes? Blue was 15.

The "box"

Not long after his mother's death, Tim Allard, Blue's best friend in whose mother's garage Blue was living, told him that nobody in Kalamazoo wanted to be around him anymore. "Why don't you just leave?" Tim said. It sounded like a good idea to Blue, so one day he backed his old pickup truck to the garage door, loaded up his motorcycle and stereo, and headed south to Houston, Texas. It was 1973.

What he called his pickup truck needs some explanation. It might even be considered one of the early motor homes that began to appear on the US recreational vehicle market in the late '60s. Blue's RV, however, looked more like the pre-WW1 German or French *Caravans,* as they were called.

Picture this...

On the bed of his red, rusting, 1968 Ford, ¾-ton pickup, he built a huge wooden box. It was 10 feet long by 7 ½ feet wide (the maximum width a highway-driven vehicle was allowed to be). In it he had a bed, a shower, a toilet, and cooking facilities—all the comforts he needed for his trip south. He even cut the roof of the cab out so he could stand up and climb back into the *box* without having to go outside.

What an incredible *box* this was! Blue's own self-built RV—a sight to behold. It included a ramp up the side, onto which Blue could wheel his "750 water-cooled Suzuki" bike that was nicknamed the *Water Buffalo.*

As for meals on the way to Houston? He cooked, which was something he would do for years, not only for himself, but for anyone who might be nearby, in trailer parks or parking lots. Blue might be called one of the original "Tailgate Chefs." He did not know at the time that this was but preparation for what would one day become a part of his ministry.

Houston in two days

"When I say I couldn't read," says Blue, "I really could read simple things like, stop, yield, speed limit, 'whopper,' and stuff like that, so as I was entering the city of Houston and saw a banner spread over the highway that said, *Love you Blue.* I thought they were welcoming me home. I didn't know the banner was for the Houston Oilers. I just knew that this was the town I was supposed to be in."

There were a lot of construction jobs available in Houston back then. They were building about 3,000 houses a week. But, even with plenty to occupy his time, there was no change in the loneliness Blue was experiencing. Every day was the same. He looked for his drugs. He looked for people to use, and he soon found that when you use people, you end up alone.

From box to bus

Blue eventually traded in his "truck with box" and motorcycle for a 1952 yellow *International School Bus.* He removed all the seats, and since no individual could personally own or drive a "yellow" school bus, he had to paint it. And paint it he did—six shades of blue, and across each side he put, **Blue's Berserko Bus.** He knew what the word berserk meant so, not lacking in creativity, he coined the word, **berserko.** He felt that was what best described who he was. He does not recall, however, how he actually spelled it, though it would have been close enough for people to understand what he meant.

Blue's Berserko Bus

Since a 6' 2" man can't stand up in a 1952 International school bus, Blue cut a hole in the floor, lowered a 55-gallon drum into the opening, and had him a sunken shower, curtain and all. And there was one other place in the bus where he could stand erect—under the sunroof he installed. Anywhere else on the bus, he had to bend over. He did that for 9 ½ years. He lived in that bus, traveled from coast to coast in that bus—to California, Washington, DC, Florida, all over the place, but he would always eventually return to Texas where he knew he could find work.

In addition to the availability of work, there was another reason Blue kept migrating back to the Houston area. All through the '70s and '80s there was a place called *Triangle Research* where "look-alike" drugs were manufactured. They made *Black Mollies,*[4] *Quaaludes,*[5] all kinds of stuff that looked like the real thing, but were totally useless.

"I would sell that stuff as the real thing," confesses Blue. "It was a good money-maker, and until the mid '80s, it was not a crime to call something cocaine that really wasn't. But when

---

[4] Street language for amphetamines
[5] Hypnotic drug popular in the '60s and '70s

the law changed, it became a crime to call a placebo by the name of any illegal drug. They would arrest you.

"Before then, however, I could crush up two aspirins and sell it as cocaine, and if I got caught by the police there was nothing they could do to me. It's not like that now. You better not even pretend or they'll get you. Though it may just be aspirin, to pretend it's cocaine is a crime. It's that serious. But when I was doing it, all I had to do was make sure I didn't run across any of the drug addicts I had sold the aspirin to."

Blue parked the bus anywhere and everywhere when he was on the road—filling stations, Walmart parking lots, grocery stores, malls, you name it. When he was in Houston, however, there were two campgrounds that he used most of the time. One was *Lake Houston State Park* where any camper could stay for 30 days. They had water, some electricity hookups, and a dump site located nearby. But at the end of 30 days you had to vacate the park and stay away for two weeks before they'd let you return.

The other campground was *Spring Creek Park* in Tomball, Texas. It operated the same way, so Blue simply moved his bus back and forth between the two, and he always had his 3-wheeler with which to get around. And wherever he went, the German shepherds were not far behind—in their van seats!

When the *Spring Creek Park* eventually changed its policy, and Blue had to move on, he didn't have far to go. There was an old farmer who had some pasture land across the road from the park, so one day Blue drove over to see him. He'd noticed that the farmer had had a trailer parked on one corner of his land, and though it was no longer there, Blue figured there would still be water and electrical hookups available. H e also figured that this farmer must be a churchgoer, or at least every Sunday morning he went somewhere, and it probably was to church. So, what does a con-artist like to do to get what he wants? Blue decided to use the spiritual approach—He decided to con the farmer by using God on him.

"Morning, sir. My name is Blue. The Lord told me to come over here to see if you would rent me that corner of your field, the one that's fenced off where you used to have a house trailer. I'll be glad to pay you $100 a month."

"I believe I can do that," the farmer said. "$100 a month and you can hook up to the water and electricity outlets."

What a deal! All Blue now had to do was drive the bus across the street and hook up to the utility connections. He knew the electric bill wouldn't be high because he had his own 6-volt batteries hooked up to the bus. He now had his own private space, and it even had a fence around it. He was ready to go on living—living, just as lonely as he'd ever been.

2

Loneliness

Loneliness was my own greatest fear, a fear that I couldn't run away from—Duane Blue

Blue now realizes that **loneliness** was probably the main thing that drove his mother over the edge. She had her workmates at the post office, but she never spent any time with them away from work. Her husband had left her almost destitute, and then there were her two sons who, rather than helping her, contributed to her loneliness. And it was this same sense of loneliness that Blue feared the most.

In the haunting song, *Eleanor Rigby,* written by the Beatles in 1966, they repeatedly ask the question,

> *"All the lonely people, where do they all come from?*
> *All the lonely people, where do they all belong?"*

Mother Teresa[6] is credited with saying, "The most terrible poverty is loneliness; the feeling of being unloved."

John Milton, English poet of the 18th century, wrote, "Loneliness is the first thing which God's eye named '<u>not good</u>.' He said, 'It is **not good** that man should be alone.'"

Someone has said that "Loneliness is not just the absence of affection, but the absence of direction."

This pretty well sums up Blue's life until he was saved at the age of 33. He had no direction or significant purpose, and

---

[6] Albanian-born missionary to India, and founder of *The Missionaries of Charity* in 1950

the loneliness he had seen in his mother's life became his own greatest fear, a fear from which he couldn't run.

The curse of loneliness

"It was almost like my mother had passed it down to me—kinda like it talks about in Deuteronomy 5:9.[7] I tried to escape my fear of loneliness by using drugs, alcohol, by using people, the campfire, the dogs, anything to fill that void," recalls Blue. "I used anything to get attention, anything to involve people in my life though, whoever it was and wherever it was, I would soon burn any relationship, abuse any friendship, until there was nothing left but ashes. Then I would just move on. To me, life was going to always be moving to a new place, making a new start."

Part of Blue's new start was his plan to eventually graduate to a double-decker bus. He thought he'd then really have a home! Though that was his long-term dream, all the time he was trying to hide from the fear of loneliness—anything he could do to hide from himself.

The problem was, wherever he went, he was with himself. He couldn't escape from Blue.

The *alone* game

"I hated me. Everybody hated me. I was a thief, a liar, a con-artist, a jerk. I didn't care about anybody but myself, and the problem was I couldn't stand myself. In that kind of lifestyle you always end up alone. It was kind of a game, a game that many people play today. We see this so often—people playing that kind of game with their lives, living in denial of what is really happening.

"This is especially true with drug people. You can never believe a drug addict. They will lie to you even when the truth is obvious. They can't help but lie. They lie because they are

---

[7] *"You shall not worship them (other gods) or serve them, for I, the Lord your God, am a jealous God, visiting the iniquity of the fathers on the children, and on the third and fourth generation of those who hate me."*

scared of being vulnerable. They don't want to take the chance that someone will find out what's really going on."

Being alone

Loneliness is not the same as just being alone. Many people have times when they are alone, through circumstances or choice. **Being alone** can be used as a positive, spiritually refreshing time, if the individual has made a conscious choice to be alone. **Loneliness,** on the other hand, is unwanted solitude and does not require being alone, because it is often experienced even in crowded places. Loneliness can be described as feeling isolated from other individuals, regardless of whether or not you are actually physically isolated from them.

Blue was around plenty of people when he worked, or when he was in the bars that he frequented almost every night. He had his drinking buddies. He was acquainted with folk in the drug scene; he could get high on cocaine or marijuana, but none of this offered any escape from the gnawing sense of being alone. The bus provided his own personal retreat where he could get stoned, but there was no retreat from loneliness. It was always waiting at the end of every "high."

And there are millions today who find themselves facing that same reality every morning they awaken, no matter how busy life may be—*"I'm alone!"* Polls indicate that the average American has fewer than two friends, and that 25% of Americans have no friends at all. This means that if you are looking at four people, one of them has no friends, period.

This describes Blue, up to the day he surrendered his life to the Lord Jesus. He had no friends, and being part of a family, or knowing the feeling of belonging, was something he had not even dared dream about.

3

A Christmas Weirdo

"Don't bring any of your weirdos home this year.
I've got one for you."

Iris' brother, Ernest, whom the family called Jug, did a double-take when he saw who he would be working with on the house-painting job he had contracted to do. Riding up on a motor-trike, with a boom-box blaring loud enough to be heard two blocks away, was this character with a beard down to the middle of his chest, hair down to his waist, with two large German shepherds sitting in two van seats behind him. Climbing off his 3-wheeler, in a voice almost as loud as the boom-box, he said: "Call me Blue." Then, looking at the dogs, he ordered: "Stay!"

Ernest later learned that this 3-wheel creation, powered by a VW engine, had been built by Blue from the ground up, and it would not be long before Ernest would learn a lot more about the intimidating figure. He learned that he could barely read or write, that he lived with his dogs in a converted school bus, that he had a checkered past of crime and drugs, that he had no real friends, that he was strong as an ox, that he was an arm-wrestler and that he had lost only one match in his life. He also discovered that Blue was constantly trying to prove he was a man, by intimidation or in just being better in something than anybody else was.

"Maybe I can't read or write, but I can hurt you better than you can hurt me," was his philosophy. Yet, in spite of all the tough show on the outside, Blue was very lonely. He was hurting on the inside, though he would never have admitted it.

The annual Yuletide guest

For several years it had been Iris' practice to invite an "unconventional" guest to join the Pat Urrey family for Christmas. These guests were always folk she had met on her travels. Among them had been one of America's top male models, who also was one of the leaders of the gay-lesbian movement in New York City.[8]

This year, however, Ernest, who called his sisters' guests, "weirdos," phoned Iris to tell her that he had found a prize one in the person of Duane Blue. "Don't you bring any of your weirdos home for Christmas this year. I've got one for you as weird as they come. He's working a house-painting job with me."

In order to interest Blue in joining the Urrey family for Christmas, Ernest had told him that he had a sister he'd like him to meet who "used to be a thief and a liar just like you." He told him about Iris' colorful past, a life Ernest felt Blue could identify with.

Christmas in (the) Rye

The tradition in the Urrey home was to have the gift exchanging on Christmas Eve, so on December 24, 1983, aboard the trike, Blue and the dogs headed for *Rye, Texas*, a town northeast of Houston, not far from *Outlaw Bend* next to *Hoop 'N Holler* and *Cut N' Shoot,* and about 75 miles from Tomball where Blue's bus was parked. Little did Blue realize that this less-than-two-hour trip from Tomball to Rye would be the beginning of a journey that would eventually change his life forever.

Blue just knew he was going to freak the Urrey family out, and especially Iris. At least that's what he expected. But that was before he had met Mirrell Urrey. No sooner had he stepped on the porch than the door opened and he found himself in the

---

[8] Read more of the Sammy Barrett story in *Iris: Trophy of Grace* available from www.duaneandIrisblue.com or www.ronowensbooks.com

embrace of the most extraordinary woman he had ever encountered. He had never been hugged before by anyone! Then to his surprise the rest of the family didn't react to his "mountain-man" figure either—in fact, they acted as though nothing was out of the ordinary. "What on earth," he thought.

He soon found himself in the middle of a praise-singing time. They sang carols and hymns and they shared testimonies about how good God was and how blessed they were as a family. Having never experienced anything like that before, Blue was getting more and more uncomfortable, but finally that came to an end and Mirrell Urrey announced that it was gift-exchanging time. As she gathered the grandchildren around her, she explained that it was their tradition to give the first gift to their "honored" guest. She handed Blue his present.

Lashing out

He opened his gift. It was *The Bible on Cassette*. Blue's reaction was one they could never have anticipated. He lashed out at Ernest, accusing him of telling everybody that he couldn't read. He was angry. As far as he was concerned, all they were doing was making him look stupid. He thought that the only reason the Bible was recorded was for people who couldn't read. He was insulted. From that point on the evening headed downhill. All Blue knew to do was to hit back, which was the kind of thing he had done all his life. He had never been able to trust anyone, and he was now convinced these folk were not any different.

"They're going to be sorry they messed with me," he said to himself, as he moved over to sit beside Iris. "Hey sister, I know all about you. You're a heroin addict, a prostitute, you've had dozens of abortions, you've slept with the Bandidos, you've been in prison for years..." Blue recalls calling her every filthy name he could think of.

"I did everything I could to hurt her, expecting her to break down in tears, but when I got through she just smiled and said, 'Yep, that's my story, and I'm going to share it at church next

Sunday morning. Why don't you go with me? You don't know half of what I've done.'

"What's gone wrong?" thought Blue. "This woman is crazy. She wants me to go to church with her! Well, I guess I might as well go and freak her out there, since I can't do it here."

Church!

Blue began putting together his "freak-Iris-out" strategy. He decided to wear his dirtiest blue jeans and the t-shirt that had all the holes in it. He went shopping on Saturday for a plastic bird to put in his beard because he wanted to look as stupid as he could when she came to pick him up. He was sure that this would so turn her off that she would not want him to go with her. Was he in for another surprise!

As Iris pulled up in her car, Blue stepped out of the bus, looking as ridiculous as a body could look, the German shepherds right behind him, plus a litter of their "babies." But instead of reacting, Iris didn't blink an eye. "Do you have a refrigerator in there?" she asked. "How do you get water? Do you have a bedroom?"

"This is crazy. This woman is acting as though there's nothing wrong with me. I can't shock her," Blue still didn't think, however, that she would take him to church looking like he did.

"OK lady. Let's go." To his amazement, she said, "Get in the car." Before he could process what was happening he found himself walking into a church for the first time in his life.

Not your normal visitor

The ushers were expecting Iris Urrey that morning, the young lady who was to give her testimony. But who was this creature with her?! She introduced Blue to the ushers, then began walking down the aisle with him in tow. As those who were already seated saw this unusual twosome heading for the front row, Blue says that it sounded as though some of them were having an asthma attack. They had never seen anything quite like this in "their" church. Though Blue was feeling a bit uncomfortable, he also knew he was shocking the crowd, and he loved it. Then, suddenly, out from one of the rows, stepped this little old blue-haired granny who barely came up to his waist. Before he knew what was happening she was giving him a hug.

"We're so glad to see you." Blue looked down at her and thought, "This woman is stoned out of her mind. I wish I had whatever she's smoking. This old lady's got a buzz on if she's glad to see me. Either that, or she's a fruitcake." She looked up at him, smiling from ear to ear, as Blue pulled himself away to follow Iris down to the front pew.

What he didn't realize was that this little white-haired lady really was high, but it was on something that Blue would not know anything about until months later. She wasn't high on anything of this world; she was high on the Holy Spirit who prompted her to reach out in love to this "strange being" who had come to church.

After the first part of the service was over, which was something he had not experienced before, Iris was introduced as the guest speaker. She got up and began sharing about her past life of crime, and all the illegal things she had been involved in. Blue couldn't believe his ears. "You fool," he thought. "You don't have to tell them the truth. Lie to them. Nobody can prove any of the crimes you committed. You've got to be the stupidest woman alive. You look like an idiot." But by the time she had finished a number of people had come forward to kneel at the altar.

The pastor then got up and said: "If anyone here is a sinner..." "Duh," thought Blue. "Who isn't?"

The pastor continued, glancing in Blue's direction; "Do you want to spend eternity in heaven or hell?"

"Now, there's a real no-brainer," Blue said to himself. "Who's going to stand up and say, 'I want to go to hell.'" When the pastor finally asked all the sinners to pray a prayer after him, Blue joined in. It was actually a prayer he had prayed before in jail, when a visiting group, or preacher, had come to speak to the prisoners. But it had never meant anything to him.

After church

At the close of the service, while the pastor and others were thanking Iris for her ministry, a few hesitant church members approached Blue, not knowing exactly what to say or do. Though he was feeling as uncomfortable as they were, he was still enjoying the thought that he probably was really freaking some of them out. If he couldn't do it to Iris, he could at least do it to them. He was correct.

Driving back to the bus, Blue told Iris that he had prayed the prayer. She didn't say anything until he was getting out of the car.

"If you think you are saved, you're not. You didn't meet Christ this morning and I don't want to leave here with you thinking that you did. You're lost. But, if you ever want to find out what it means to know Christ, you phone me collect, any time of the day or night. I live in Atlanta. Here's my phone number."

Iris handed him her calling card and drove off. Blue thought, "That's the last time I'll ever see her." What he did not realize at that moment was that God the Father, through the work of the Holy Spirit, was in the process of drawing this lonely, hurting rebel to His Son, the Lord Jesus.

4

The Hound of Heaven[9]

Back in the bus Blue tried to process what had just happened. It had been six days since his *Christmas with the Urreys'* experience, when he had not been able to shock or turn the family off. Now, on Sunday, after thinking he could freak Iris out by looking as stupid as he could, she had turned the tables on him. She had challenged him to call her, at her expense, to find out what it really means to be a Christian.

For 9 ½ years he had retreated to the security of his bus. His booze, drugs and dogs were all that he had needed. Now he was beginning to have questions. He was wondering why he even wanted to talk to Iris again. Why was he now wanting to know more about this Christian thing? Was it because he had just met real ones for the first time in his life? Yes, but more importantly, and something Blue could not be aware of, God was pursuing him, in spite of the degenerate lifestyle he had been living for years.

The picture of God's pursuit of a lost soul, as we find portrayed in Francis Thompson's famous poem, *The Hound of Heaven,* well describes what was happening in Blue's life at that moment. He had been running and running for years, not allowing anyone to get through the façade behind which he was

---

[9] Francis Thompson, (1859 – 1907) was an <u>English</u> poet whose writings, *The Hound of Heaven* in particular, profoundly touched a young J. R. R. Tolkien, who said that Thompson had a major influence on his own writing. Thompson's poetry came out of deep personal adversity and self-willfulness, during which he became increasingly aware that his soul was being pursued by a caring and loving God whom he described as *The Hound of Heaven.*

living. Every day he needed to prove just how tough and in control he was, while drowning himself in drugs and alcohol that helped support his life of make-believe.

The midnight call

There were no cell phones in January 1984, so when Blue decided to take Iris up on her offer to have him call her collect, he had to go to the nearest phone booth that was located across the street in Spring Street Mobile Home Park where he used to park his bus. Being a night-owl, which is not uncommon for those who live the kind of lifestyle Blue was living, he placed the call around midnight, Central Standard Time, which was 1 AM in Atlanta. When he dialed zero for the operator, he had no idea what to expect. Would Iris accept his call? Would she even remember who he was?

"Operator, I want to make a collect call to Iris Urrey in Atlanta, Georgia, at 770-536-9213."
"Sir, who is it from?"
"Oh…tell her it's from Blue in Texas.
 R-i-n-g…R-i-n-g…
"Iris Urrey?"
"Yes."
"You have a collect call from Blue in Tomball, Texas. Will you accept?"
Blue's heart was racing.
"Yes I will. I've been praying he would call."

And so the calls began. When she was home, Iris didn't know when the phone might ring. Sometimes it was in the wee hours of the morning. At first Blue called twice a week, then, almost every night.

Blue looks back

"What freaked me out most about Iris was that she was so transparent," remembers Blue. "She could read anybody who tried to fake it. I'll never forget what happened during one of those early collect phone calls in the middle of the night. I told her that I was really thinking about selling my bus and getting a house. She didn't pause a second. "You're lying. You'll never sell your bus. It's your security and you can always leave when you get into trouble. You're going to just end up lonely and miserable."

"I hated her for that because I knew she was exactly right, but I wasn't ready to admit it. She was the first person in my whole life I felt I couldn't fool.

"I told her one time how I had gotten intimidated over a roofing project. Later, after I had been saved, she told me that when people made me feel stupid I would fight back by intimidating them. And she was exactly right. That was what I had done my whole life. She said that I had tried to convince people that I was stupid and that I had been real good at it. I thought, 'Wow, lady. That's true. Why couldn't I have ever seen that?'"

These collect calls went on for over two months. Blue was trying to wear Iris down. He was testing her. One month her phone bill exceeded $700. Glenn Sheppard, who oversaw her ministry at the Home Mission Board of the Southern Baptist Convention, tried to get her to refuse what he thought were an excessive number of collect calls from Texas. Iris wouldn't cooperate so he finally had her phone disconnected. To get it reconnected it was going to cost her $500.

Her next ministry engagement, after the phone was disconnected, was at Park Avenue Baptist Church in Titusville, Florida, where her friend, Peter Lord, was pastor. She was there to share her testimony and to be a part of their Wednesday night prayer service. She asked the congregation to pray for the conversion of someone in Texas by the name of Blue. After she had told them what she knew about him, over 700 people spontaneously stood to their feet and began to intercede for this Blue.

"It sounded like a rushing wind," recalls Iris. And above the symphony of prayers she would occasionally hear, "Oh God, save Blue. Oh God, tear down the stronghold of Satan in his life. Oh God, save Blue."

The countdown continues

Iris flew home that night on a "red-eye" flight, arriving in Atlanta at 3:30 AM. As she opened her apartment door the phone was ringing. "But it's been disconnected," she thought. "How can it be ringing?" What Iris didn't know was that when Glenn Sheppard had told some of her friends about his having to cut her phone off to teach her a lesson, a woman in Conyers took it upon herself to pay the $500 deposit and have the phone reconnected while Iris was in Florida.

Iris knew who it had to be when she picked up the receiver. It was Blue. The first thing she heard was, "I prayed to receive Jesus tonight." That didn't impress Iris any more than what he had told her he had done in that church service more than two months before. She was not going to make it easy on him.

No easy road

Iris began questioning the genuineness of his confession. "Where were you tonight at 7 o'clock?" That would have been 8 PM Eastern time in Titusville, Florida, when the church was praying.

He said, "I was where I am every night; at the Brown Road Tavern. I smoked some dope in the parking lot, then went inside and drank rum and coke."

Blue continued: "Iris, I've decided to sell my bus and buy a house."

"You already told me that, and no, you're not going to sell it because you're just going to keep driving around in that prison cell of yours."

This made Blue angry. "Look lady. You don't know who you're dealing with."

Iris: "Don't you get angry with me and try to prove you're a tough guy. You're nothing but a punk."

Blue: "If I could reach through this telephone I'd choke you."

The net tightens

"Before you try to prove how macho you are with me one more time, I've got a question to ask you. What would you do right now if you were standing in a church and a beautiful girl in a white dress said she was going to marry you and the preacher would look at you and ask, 'Do you want to take this woman as your wife?' You would say 'I do,' in front of witnesses. That's the law of our country.

"But what would you do if, when the preacher asked the woman if she would take you, she smiled and said: 'I want to spend the rest of my life with Blue. I love him so much and I want to be his wife, but I'm going to sleep with Tim every Friday night because I've dated him for years and it's become a habit. But after I sleep with him on Fridays, I'll go back to Blue and be his wife the rest of the time.'"

"Lady, you're crazy. I'd never marry anybody who's sleeping around with someone else."

Blue then began cussing and yelling. When he had cooled down, Iris said: "You mean, you wouldn't accept her commitment?" Blue yelled, "That's no commitment. That's a bunch of garbage."

Rather than retreating from Blue's "intimidation technique" that he had so often used over the years to either win an argument or put someone down, Iris said: "What do you think God is going to do with the commitment you said you made tonight?"

In that moment, Blue began to understand where Iris was going. She was helping him understand that salvation is more than just saying words, like a lot of people have done; it is a change of life. It's leaving the old life behind and turning to go in a completely new direction.

Captured by God's love

"I think I understand." After a long pause, he said: "I want to pray." Iris was beginning to hear what she had been waiting to hear for two months. "Alright," she said.

Standing in a phone booth, almost a thousand miles away, Blue waited for Iris to lead him in a prayer. But there was nothing but silence. Iris didn't say a thing. He waited and she still didn't say anything. He kept waiting. His stomach began churning. Suddenly he was doing something he had never done in his life—he was crying. Through the tears Iris heard him say:

"I don't know how to talk to God. All I know is that I'm sick and tired of the life I've been living and if God can do anything with me, I'll do anything He asks me to do."

In his testimony Blue says that that perhaps wasn't the usual Baptist prayer you hear, but it was one that came from his heart, and God heard it. He had been captured by God's love. He'd never look back.

Section Two

A New Start

"I have been made a New Creation,
with Christ I have been crucified.
And what I was I am no longer
because I died when Jesus died.
I can't explain, it is a mystery,
I don't know how it can be true.
I just accept what He's accomplished,
I'm born again, all things are new!"[10]

---

[10] From the song, *New Creation*. Words by Ron Owens.

5

A New Creation

"If anyone is in Christ, he is a new creation; old things have passed away; behold, all things have become new"
(11 Corinthians 5:17 NKJV).

The transaction that took place in the wee hours of that March 17 morning, 1984, was immediately evident. Blue did not wait a day or two to process what he had experienced; he had made an about-face and he was ready to take off.

It blew his mind that a 33-year-old man, living in a bus for almost 10 years, who knew nothing about Jesus, who only knew how to act mean, lie, steal, cheat people, and who didn't care about anything in the world except himself, that someone who knew everything he had ever done, called his name. "Duane Blue, I died for you. I love you!"

The morning the dog's names changed
"Hey, Fatty. Load up, Skinny." Blue's two German Shepherds weren't sure he was talking to them because for years he had been calling them by the female "B#" name for dogs.

These were "one-man" dogs that had lived with Blue seven of the nine and a half years he lived on the bus. Before he had *Fatty* and *Skinny,* he had owned a big white shepherd he named Arthur Fonzerelli. He trained him to ride on a 2-wheel motorcycle. Fonzerelli got run over in Indiana. Fatty and Skinny were trained to ride on the 3-wheel motor-trike. They each had their own seat, right behind Blue—two van seats welded together.

On your mark, get set, witness!

"For with the heart one believes unto righteousness, and with the mouth confession is made unto salvation" (Romans 10:10 NKJV).

Blue didn't have to be told that he needed to tell others about what had happened—it was the first thing he wanted to do. When he returned to the bus he knew that he had to let his work-buddies know what had happened. He knew he needed to begin cutting ties with his past life so, after flushing all his drugs and booze down the toilet, and as soon as *Fatty* and *Skinny* had taken their seats, Blue took off with the big, thick, green, hardbound King James Bible that Iris had sent him, tied to the front of his 3-wheeler.

"We've got to tell those creeps at the job what happened last night," he hollered back to the dogs, as all three sped down the freeway, hair blowing in the wind. They were headed for Lake Houston, 30 miles away, and the job site where he had been working.

When Blue arrived, he snapped his fingers at the dogs again. "Stay." They did, just as they were trained to do. Blue never had to take the key out of the ignition, and he never had a theft problem. No one had ever dared approach his 3-wheeler. If they had, they would have ended up with at least one less appendage. Blue walked up on the job site, waving that big green Bible.

"I've come this morning to tell you all that I'm quitting. I can't work with a bunch of lying, thieving jerks like you. I'm going to church because I met Jesus early this morning. You creeps ought to come to church too. There's plenty of them around. I'm going to go and find one."

Without waiting for a reaction, he turned, ordered the dogs to take their seats again, jumped on the trike, and went looking for a church. He wanted to find one near where he lived so he drove the 30 miles back across town. He went right past where his bus was parked, where Brown Road turns down to the Spring Creek Park, and turned into the first church he saw.

Now, Blue didn't know one church from the other back then. He didn't know that churches are different, but he was to soon find out that they are. The first one he stopped at didn't exactly welcome him with open arms. He knocked on the door. A man in a suit answered. When he saw Blue it sounded like he was having an asthma attack. Blue said:

"Man, I just met Jesus and I'm coming here to church." The man in the suit, who may have been the pastor, said, "No you're not. In fact, please leave and take your dogs with you. I want you off this property right now."

Blue wasn't phased at all. "Cool," he said to himself, as he climbed back on his 3-wheeler with *Fatty* and *Skinny* and his big green King James Bible. "There are plenty of other churches," and, providentially, the next one turned out to be Central Baptist Church, the one Iris had told him about, where her friend, Charles Bullock, was pastor.

Central Baptist had a Christian school and there must have been 100 or more kids running around when this big ugly thing, with hair and a beard down to his waist, climbed off his trike, snapped his fingers at two mean-looking dogs and shouted, "Stay!" He then walked into the building where he ran right into the pastor. Blue remembers Charles Bullock's response to what was standing in front of him:

"Do you need gas or food?"
"No sir, I just met Jesus and I need to find out more about Him. Are you the pastor?"
"Yes."
"Good. You can call me Blue, and wherever you go, I'm going."
"I'm sorry, but you can't do that," he said. "I've got two hospital visits to make this morning."

"Great! Where's your car?"

"No," he said. "You don't understand. I've got two hospitals to go to. I'm going to be visiting sick people. After that I'm meeting some preachers for lunch, then this afternoon I have to go to the bookstore."

"Cool," said Blue.

He then walked out to the parking lot, reminded *Fatty* and *Skinny* that they were to "stay," then he climbed into the only car that was sitting near the church office door. He waited. Finally the pastor came. Blue could tell that he was really freaked out when he saw who was sitting in the back seat. But, he probably was more afraid of upsetting his passenger. As he headed for the hospital he wondered how he was going to explain this hairy dude sitting behind him in the back seat.

At the first hospital "they" visited two people. The pastor explained to each patient that Blue had just come to the church that morning and that he wanted to learn about being a Christian. They went to the next hospital where the same thing happened. Then they went to lunch.

"You should have seen the look on the faces of those four pastors when we walked in," recalls Blue. "As I sat down at their table they also looked like they were on the verge of an asthma attack."

Before the pastor could say anything, Blue said: "Hi, I just got saved. I gave my life to Jesus last night and I don't know anybody around here that's a Christian except him." Pointing to the preacher, he said: "What did you say your name is?"

When they got back to the church Blue asked, "What time do you start in the morning?"

The pastor said, "Well, I get here by 8 o'clock."

Blue said, "Me too. I quit my job, I own my house and those two dogs. I ain't got no debt and probably have around $700 to live on. I can go a couple months without working so I'll be here every day to learn about Jesus and help around the church any way I can."

When Blue arrived the next morning Charles Bullock said: "You know, our janitor is texturing the bathroom this morning and he probably could use some help. Come and let me introduce you to him."

To me, he was pure Jesus

He led Blue down the hallway to meet Bobby Conners, who turned out to be one of the godliest men Blue has ever met.

"I learned so much from him," recalls Blue. "And he became one of my closest friends. He still is. He never went to seminary. He had been a factory worker and a drug addict, but he knew God's Word, and lived it like few people I've ever known. To me, he was pure Jesus."

Bobby said: "If we're going to work together, let's go sit in my office and get acquainted." Blue followed him down the hall where he opened a door and said: "Welcome to my office. Grab a bucket and sit down." They were in a 4- by 6-foot storage closet with brooms, mops, all kinds of janitorial stuff.

Blue thought, "Man, this guy is messed up. He calls this his office?"

"What do you think?" Bobby asked.

"What am I going to say?" Blue thought. "You're crazy? This ain't no office!"

Bobby started talking about Jesus. "We're going to texture the bathroom for Jesus," he said. "We're going to replace the drywall for Jesus. We're going to do this for Jesus. We're going to do that for Jesus."

Blue told him that he had all kinds of tools in his bus, including a texturing machine. "I ended up bringing my equipment to the church where me and Bobby spent hours a day working together on all kinds of projects. This went on for over a year, until me and Iris got married."

Bobby remained the janitor at Central Baptist, Pinehurst, for two more years before starting a church in his home. This led to renting space in a strip mall and eventually to purchasing property and building a building, all by faith, without borrowing any money. He had been greatly influenced by Brother Manley Beasley who taught him, as he had Blue and Iris, about the faith life. Bobby felt that it didn't make sense to ask man for something when he could go to his heavenly Father who owned everything.

6

A Lesson from Miss Alice

Before he was saved, Blue spent most of his evenings at the Brown Road Tavern in Tomball, Texas. His favorite drink was rum and coke—he would bring the rum and buy the coke. Often, however, before going inside, there was drug dealing in the parking lot.

Miss Alice and her three beers

She knew all the guys who frequented the bar. She would show up every evening for an hour and a half and drink three beers—not two and not four. Always three; then she went home.

An interesting bond developed between the guys and Miss Alice. They loved her and she loved them, as friends, though Blue never learned her full name and didn't have any idea who she really was or where she lived. She was just Miss Alice.

When Blue tried to buy her a beer one night he discovered that she had already prepaid for 12, which would take her through the next four nights.

Every Friday night she would bring a five-gallon bucket of either chili or spaghetti, and serve everyone a bowl, free. Sometimes she fed as many as 50 guys, every Friday night. "We loved that old lady," recalls Blue, "but we didn't know who she was and she didn't know us."

When Blue got saved he stopped going to the bar, and after two weeks, who should show up at his Berserko Bus, but Miss Alice. She had noticed that he hadn't been at the bar and wondered if he was alright. She told him that she had heard that he had quit his job, and guessed that he didn't have any money, so she had brought him a bottle of rum and a little pot of soup. She said if he would come back to the bar she would buy him a drink. She said, "I just wanted to know if you were OK."

Blue said: **"Miss Alice, the man you came to visit doesn't live here no more. He died two weeks ago.** I can show you a picture of his funeral.[11] They buried him and I was raised in his place. I now live here in this bus with Jesus and that creep you used to see at the bar ain't coming back no more. You'll never see him again."

A "Miss Alice" lesson

It had rained real hard the fifth Sunday after Blue joined the church and his 3-wheeler refused to start, so he didn't make it to church either Sunday morning or Sunday night.

"I thought that since the bar had come looking for me after two weeks' absence that someone from the church would phone or come by to check on me, but they didn't. Perhaps if I had missed another Sunday they would have, but I'm not sure, because many churches don't have time to check on their sheep."

An indictment

"Within three miles of my mother's house were eight different kinds of churches. We lived in that house on Alcott Street in Kalamazoo, Michigan, for over seven years. Seven years, and not once did anyone knock on our door to tell my mother about Jesus. And the very moment she died on that linoleum floor, she went to hell. Not a church in Kalamazoo cared for her soul.

"I tell people that they can be sure that the world is going to come after their kids, but the church, that has the greatest message of all, so often fails to seek after the lost.

"What happens to many saved people is that they become like magicians. Magicians aren't supposed to tell their secrets,

---

[11] Blue had had a picture taken of his baptism the week before.

and that's the way many Christians act. They take their salvation home, sit it on their mantel where they can look at it and be reminded that they've got it. They're headed for streets of gold one day, and they never tell a single soul about how to go to heaven."

The clock of life is wound but once,
and no one has the power,
To tell just when the hands will stop,
at late or early hour.
To lose one's wealth is sad indeed,
to lose one's health is more. BUT—
To lose one's soul is such a loss,
that no one can restore.
—Robert H. Smith[12]

---

[12] Unsuccessful attempts have been made to find copyright information for this poem.

7

A Vacation Fit for a Robot

Dead and buried

Blue couldn't believe what he was hearing when his pastor, Charles Bullock, described the meaning of water baptism.

"Baptism is a picture of all the sin and junk of your past life being buried in a watery grave, and that when you are raised up, out of the water, it is a picture of being raised to live a new life in Jesus Christ."

Blue almost tackled Bro. Charles: "I want that right away, and I want someone to take a picture of that creep being buried because he's not alive any more. He doesn't live on my bus anymore. He's dead."

Ready for anything, except...

From the moment he was saved, Blue became the church's No. 1 volunteer for anything that needed to be done at church. Initially, however, because of his unkempt appearance (long beard and hair), no one wanted to sit near him. That didn't faze Blue. Every time the preacher asked for volunteers his was the first hand raised, that is, for everything except the nursery. "I ain't doing that," he'd say to himself. Having spent little or no time around children, he actually was intimidated by them.

One Saturday night, sitting in the bus, Blue told the Lord that whatever volunteers the preacher asked for on Sunday morning he was going to offer to help. And wouldn't you know it, the request was for nursery helpers! Blue just sat there, frozen, on the front row. They sang another song then the pastor asked again. They needed more. He said, "I believe there is someone sitting here right now who last night, sitting in their home, told God that they'd volunteer today."

"I was flabbergasted," recalls Blue. "How does he know that?" So, up went his hand. Seconds later, hands began to go up all over the sanctuary. Some women headed straight to the nursery. No one was about to let that bearded, long-haired, scary-looking man sitting in the front row get anywhere near their children!

Blue was broken. "God, you've got to give me another chance to do something." The pastor's next request was for 20 volunteers to work in Vacation Bible School. This time Blue didn't just raise his hand, he stood up. The pastor began counting the hands that were raised and when he had counted 12, he looked at Blue, paused for a moment, then said: "Thirteen."

The surprise

After the service Blue headed for the platform. "Preacher, thank you for counting me. I don't even have a suitcase and I don't know what to pack to go on vacation next week, but I'm ready. You know I can't read yet, but I'm willing to go. I'm thrilled to death, but you're going to have to help me."

The pastor started to laugh. "Blue, it's not going to be a vacation. We're going to have about 300 kids down here next week."

"Kids? What do you, mean, kids?" asked Blue. "I didn't know it had to do with kids."

They decided to put Blue in a room with four- and five-year-olds to be a "go-fer" for three ladies who would be working with them. The ladies told him that he was to do whatever they asked him to do. "OK," thought Blue. "They'll have me setting up chairs and getting drinks." Not so!

"The whole thing started at 9 o'clock," recalls Blue, "and as I watched the teachers try to get those kids under control, by 9:05 I began thinking, 'This is stupid. I've got to get out of here.

This ain't for me. I'm willing to do anything else in the church; Sunday School, worship, fix things, anything but this.'"

Blue had actually even started attending the WMU, and wondered why more men weren't there—that is until someone told him that WMU meant Women's Missionary Union!

Escape plan foiled

So, there he was, standing in the corner, wondering how he was going to escape, when one of the ladies said she had to go and get something. Blue told the other two ladies that he wasn't feeling well, and was going to have to leave also.

"I went to this lady and told her that I was sick. The problem was, I was freaking out. They asked me to stay just a bit longer and watch those kids while they went to talk to Bro. Charles. Those two ladies took off also and left me with 27 wild, four- and five-year-olds. As they left, one of the ladies pointed at me and said, 'Now, you stay right here and watch these children. Don't you leave.'"

That was when Blue began to really panic. His hands started to sweat. He backed into the corner and honestly began to think, "What if they all attack me as a group? They're little, but man, I could really get hurt. But even more scary is, what if one of these kids gets hurt? All they'll want to know is how did my child get hurt? What did that big hairy guy do to them? What would the parents do to me? The parents are going to want their kids back. They're not going to accept my telling them that they can't have their child back because he mysteriously died in Vacation Bible School."

As he stood in the corner the children started to tear the place up. They turned over furniture, they began peeling paper off the wall, eating crayons, running around, screaming and hollering. Blue knew he had to do something quick, so he stepped to the middle of the room and began to use his very loud robot voice that starts way down in his toes.

Robot to the rescue

Sounding like growling thunder, Blue said: "Hello there earth-children. I'm a robot from outer space. My name is Blue. Pick up all the crayons and put them in the box." The children froze, and for a moment they stared at him in shock. This hairy giant suddenly was shaking the room with his voice. They started picking up crayons as fast as they could. "Now, turn the tables and chairs back up." They did. "Good! Everybody stand up straight with your arms by your side." They immediately followed his order. "Don't move. No talking." No one moved. "OK, now sit down in rows." They quickly scrambled to sit in rows. They would do anything he asked them to do. He then began using his Mickey Mouse, Goofy, and Donald Duck voices.

When the ladies returned, they couldn't believe their eyes, or ears. The children were sitting there, enraptured with this hairy robot from outer space. He had not only managed to get them under control, but he had begun to win their little hearts. When the ladies took over, Blue got on the floor and joined the children in their activities. He was becoming one of them. This was the coolest thing the kids had ever experienced. And it was also one of the coolest things Blue had ever had happen in his 33 years.

"They gave us Styrofoam cups with dirt in them," remembers Blue. "Then they gave us seeds to put in the dirt. Then they told us to write our names on the cups. Now, that was a problem. I couldn't do that. I didn't know how to write, so I had one of the little kids help me. They really liked that."

By the time VBS was over that morning, Blue had bonded with the children. They all wanted him to be their friend. Some hung on to him as they were leaving, especially one little boy whose name was Zack. He took Blue's hand and asked if he would go home with him for a meal.

They walked to the parking lot where Jan, Zack's mother, was waiting. When they got to the car, Zack said: "Brudder

Blue is going to eat lunch with us today, Mommy. He's a robot." Blue and Zack climbed into the back seat.

A change of heart

Jan knew who Blue was, at least she had seen him in church, and had been quite judgmental and critical of him. Now, as she watched him interacting with her little boy she began to catch a glimpse of what was inside this hairy giant, and later, as she was serving the sandwiches, she began to cry. She asked Blue to forgive her for how she had felt toward him and for the things she had said about him. She asked how she might be a blessing to him. Blue said: "There's nothin' I need you to do for me. I'm just learning about church and Jesus."

However, when Jan discovered that Blue could barely read, she knew how she and the family could be a blessing to him. She invited him to join them several times a week for sandwiches and reading lessons. Jan and Randy, her husband, would soon become two of Blue's best friends. They studied the Bible together, and as they did, they were helping Blue learn to read, by reading Scripture.

Blue recalls having seen Randy at church, but he had not yet realized that Randy was a police officer. The first time Blue saw him in uniform Randy hugged him and thanked him for the example he was setting to him and the family in the area of witnessing. Randy had been watching Blue and had been challenged, himself, to share Jesus with more people. He said: "I figured that if God could save a con with a background like yours, He could save anybody."

Blue's response was, "Hey, Randy, you ought to thank God He was even able to save a cop!"

Occasionally Randy would take Blue in the police car with him. He'd drop him off in tough areas of town for an hour or so before coming back to pick him up. He said: "I can't stop and talk to them about Jesus. They'd run. But you can." And so, police officer and ex-conman worked together to reach the lost.

8

Anyway, Anytime, Anywhere

Anyway, anytime, anywhere Lord,
Serving You every day is my prayer.
Take me Lord, use me Lord for your glory.
Anyway, anytime, anywhere.[13]

Knowing that Blue had lived on a converted school bus for so many years, the pastor asked him to see if anything could be done with an old GMC school bus the church had that had broken down and had not been used in two years. Blue accepted the challenge, and after replacing the battery, spark plugs, wiring, and doing a good bit of tinkering, he had the bus up and running in five days.

Blue's involvement with the bus did not end with just repairing it. As he worked, he began thinking of how he might be able to use it in ministry. The bus had the church name on the side, and it could carry 30 passengers, so now, all he needed were a few others to help him with his *kids' outreach program.*

The plan was to go door to door to tell parents that, if they would be willing, a bus would be stopping by at 9 o'clock Sunday morning to pick up their children for Sunday School, and that they would be returned, safe and sound, as soon as it was over.

Brown paper bags?

But Blue's plan did not end there. After knocking on lots of doors and talking to lots of people, he took the bus and drove

---

[13] From the song, *Anyway, Anytime, Anywhere.* Words by Ron Owens

into town to shop. At a Christian bookstore he bought a bunch of Jesus' stickers. At a grocery store he loaded up on candy and bubble gum. He then got a roll each of pennies, nickels, and dimes, and 25 brown paper bags.

Blue then put a mini-roll of a dime, nickel, and penny in each of the bags, along with candy, bubble gum, and a Jesus sticker. He then prayed: "God, I'd like to have 25 kids on the bus in the morning."

A Sunday morning mess

"I picked up 19 kids. When we got to church I gave a bag to each one, praying that this would encourage them to come back to Sunday School."

Ten minutes later, with mission accomplished, Blue was sitting in his own Sunday School class when the pastor, Bro. Charles, came to get him. "Blue, I heard about your brown paper bag idea, but let me show you what has happened."

"We walked down the hall to the area where the kids were," recalls Blue. "There were stickers all over the walls, candy wrappers all over the floors, and bubble gum stuck to everything in sight!

"'Blue, I think that your brown paper bag idea is a good one, but you are going to have to wait to pass them out when you drop the children off at their homes—then their parents can clean up after them. Speaking of cleaning up—you'll need to clean this mess up after church.'

"So, I cleaned up the room that day, and from then on I gave the kids their bags when they got off the bus."

What next?

After the bus ministry was going well, Blue turned it over to others who were ready to take the responsibility. He had seen another way he could be a blessing to his church family, and to widows and incapacitated members in particular.

"I started doing construction and painting work for widows and other members who were not well or crippled. I put a sign-up sheet on the bulletin board:

Sign up here if you need help with construction or painting, or anything else around the house.

"People started signing up for all kinds of stuff they needed done," recalls Blue. "I had a flat-bed pickup truck and I went from place to place, painting houses, building tables and chairs, and I even helped one guy pave his driveway.

"There were lots of jobs and I didn't charge *nothin'*. The only thing I asked was permission to put a sign in the yard of the house I was working in that read:

WORK BEING DONE BY A SERVANT OF JESUS CHRIST

All I wanted to do was help the family out. *Family!* That's what blows me away. *Family!* I belong to a family. God's family! And as His family He wants us to always be looking for ways we can help each other.

A Jesus deal

In addition to working for the "family," Blue would go up and down the roads bidding on jobs. He'd only charge for the material so his bids came in so low that people didn't think he was any good. The preacher had preached on restitution and Blue knew he couldn't drive around on his bus repaying everyone he had ripped off, so this was a part of making up for what he had done in his past life.

"I made a bid on a guy's house. I figured the paint would cost about $350 and that's what I bid. Another guy was there who bid $2,800. The man chose that bid. Another guy across the street heard our conversation and called out, "I've already got the paint. What will you charge to do the work?"

"Nothing," Blue replied. "I won't be doing the work for you, I'll be doing it for Jesus. The only requirement is that I can put a sign in your front yard that says,

WORK BEING DONE BY A SERVANT
OF JESUS CHRIST

Two days later, when the painters had finished with the $2,800 job across the street and had gone their way, the owner discovered that they had forgotten to paint the garage door because it was up. He asked Blue what he would charge to paint it.

"The same amount I said I'd charge to do your whole house. Nothing. I'll do it for Jesus."

A Tribute

Ruffin Snow—pastor, Tri-Cities Baptist Church
Conover, North Carolina

Every man who has felt like an outsider looking in, relates to Duane Blue. Every guy who secretly knows that he has to put on a tough front for fear someone will find out how shy or sensitive he is, can identify with Blue. When he shares his story with that dead-pan humor, then breaks out into that huge smile, everyone in the place, with any heart at all, thinks of some outcast with whom they must share the love of Jesus.

I've had the privilege of having Duane and Iris with me in churches both in Oklahoma and North Carolina, and the Lord has always used them to capture the hearts of people. There's an instant rapport.

Duane's a big biker, of course. On a ride we made through the foothills of the Blue Ridge Mountains, he was on a *Wyatt Fuller, customized Harley Davidson Fat Boy.* He is fearless! He is fearless both on the bike AND as a witness to what they call "one-percenters."

I've heard Blue say that he's not a preacher, that he's just a satisfied customer, and that's great. But he's also a bold witness where it's tough...on the street, in hostile environments, he is not intimidated. That's one of the reasons I have such respect for Duane Blue.

9

A Passion for Souls

"You shall receive power when the Holy Spirit has come upon you; and you shall be witnesses to me in Jerusalem, and in all Judea and Samaria, and to the end of the earth" (Acts 1:8 NKJV).

By being around Bobby Conners and a few other folk in the church, Blue began to really hunger for God.

"I wanted everything they had. I'd hear them say: "God told me this,' or, 'I heard God say…' so I sat for hours in my bus asking God to say something to me. 'God, tell me what to do.' I really wanted to know what God wanted me to do and I thought they were actually hearing His voice; a real voice. I wanted my life to make a difference. I had not learned yet how God speaks, but I did know that He wanted me to speak about Him."

Born to witness

Realizing what God did in reaching down to draw him out of his pit of sin, is something that Blue has never gotten over. From the moment of his conversion he has used every opportunity to let others know what Jesus has done for him, though not always in the most conventional way.

Iris, his wife and partner in ministry, says that from the moment Blue was saved, the command of our Lord to be witnesses became Blue's passion. "He doesn't wake up in the morning saying, 'I'm going to witness to someone today,' it's his lifestyle, it's just him. Wherever he is, it's as much a part of his life as saying 'hello' is to most people. Whoever he's talking to, the conversation always ends up with his telling them about Jesus."

When Blue found out that the pastor had asked Bobby Conners to head up an *Evangelism Explosion* training program at the church, he immediately signed up. Bobby knew that Blue could barely read or write, but that didn't really matter because Blue had a memory like a "steel trap-door"—whatever he heard, he remembered.

Bobby recalls the time when Mike Ballard, a plumber and Blue's *Evangelism Explosion* trainer, was being hassled for playing Christian music on a job site. Some framers on the job site began to threaten him: "Turn down that blankety-blank music or we'll make you wish you had." When Blue heard about this, he asked to go to work with Mike the next morning. Blue said: "I don't know that much about plumbing, but I'd like to go and witness to the creeps who are giving you problems."

Blue arrived the next morning with a Sandi Patti tape and his ghetto-buster. He turned the volume up to maximum and waited.

That afternoon Mike called Bobby Conners to report on what happened.

"When we got to the job site Blue cranked the music up as loud as he could. I said, 'But…' Blue said, 'Don't worry, I'll take care of it from here.' Soon the framers were coming down the hall, cussing up a storm. They shoved the door open and the biggest framer barged in. Before I knew it, Blue had grabbed him by the shirt and had him pinned against the wall. 'Hi, my name is Blue. I used to be a very violent person but I've been saved and I want to tell you about Jesus.'"

As far as we know that man did not receive Jesus as his Savior that day, but we do know that the framers never messed with this young brother again over his playing Christian radio. Charles Bullock, the pastor, later explained to Blue that that kind of "confrontational evangelism" doesn't usually bear much fruit. Blue's response to this was:

"Brother Charles, you told me about Jesus' brothers, James and Jude. I've been listening to those books on my tape recorder. It says in Jude, the smallest book in the Bible, that some would be saved by snatching them from the fire and I was just trying to snatch that guy." Charles explained that that was not really what Jude meant.

An unconventional E. E. graduate

Soon after Blue had graduated from the *Evangelism Explosion* training he went knocking on doors with Mike. Blue will never forget Roy Black.

"We knocked on the door and Mr. Black answered. At first he wasn't going to let us in until I said:

'Mr. Black, my name is Mr. Blue, and us colored folk need to stick together."

He laughed and said: 'Where did you say you people are from?'

'We're from the Baptist Church down the road and I wanted to come and tell you that Jesus loves you.'"

They were invited in. Blue went on to ask the appropriate questions and told him how he lived in a bus and had been a drug addict. He finally used the "book of sin" illustration where you take a book, representing your sin, and place it, your sin, in one hand, then you take the book and transfer it over on to the other hand as you explain how Jesus takes your sin away.

Blue asked: "Does that make sense to you, that Jesus can take away our sin?"

"Yes it does," said Roy Black.

"Do you think you'd like to receive the Lord Jesus as your Savior?"

"Yes, I would."

He answered so quickly that Blue thought something had gone wrong, so he started again.

"You need to understand that you have to repent of your sin and let God change the wrong things in your life. He is still doing that in me. And He has a lot more to change."

Mr. Black said: "I understand. I want to pray."

Blue still felt that he must have left something out, but he hadn't. They prayed. Roy Black was one of the first persons he led to the Lord.

Witnessing balloons

Bobby Conners recalls another occasion when 25 from Central Church went to Gatlinburg, Tennessee. One day, Blue, Bobby and one other man were standing on the sidewalk where hundreds of people were passing by.

"Blue reached into his pocket, took out several balloons, blew them up into the shape of an apple and gave one to each of us. He said: 'Hold the balloon up with one hand and thump it with the other.' We said, 'Blue we're going to look silly.' 'Just do it,' he said. So we did.

"As we were thumping our balloons we heard Blue call out in his very loud voice, 'Hi folks. We are part of the Moron Tap-an-Apple Choir and we want to tell you about Jesus.' A crowd formed, stopping the flow of traffic on the sidewalk, as Blue presented the Gospel right on the spot."

An unconventional opener

Knowing nothing but "confrontational" relationships from the time he was a child, at the age of 33 Blue struggled with how to relate to people, how to talk to them, how to carry on a meaningful conversation without scaring them. So, he decided to use something that we may think of as childish, that in actuality is childlike, which was a whole new world Blue was entering.

Jesus had demonstrated the heart attitude we are to have if we expect to enter the Kingdom of God when he sat a little child on His lap and said: *"Except you become as little children..."* (Matthew 18:3 KJV).

Though Blue did not yet know what Jesus had said, he instinctively turned to something that both children and adults respond to—something he could use as an opener to get people to listen to him and not run off because of his loud voice and, at times, intimidating manner.

Balloons

In restaurants, grocery stores, schools, churches, prisons, on planes, anywhere, out of his pocket Blue pulls a balloon. No, not just a balloon, but what seems to be an unending supply that is instantly transformed into poodles, humming birds, parrots, and two different kinds of swords, one of them being a visual aid representing the Word of God. This sword has a safety tip on the end which represents the blood of Jesus that points you to Calvary, and when you turn it around it becomes a cross.

Then there is Jonah and the whale, which ends up with a balloon inside of a balloon, turtles, giraffes, penguins, and the list goes on and on. In restaurants he always gives the waitress a "spoonful of love" balloon, a big spoon with a heart in it, or it might be a "heart within a heart" balloon as he explains that once you receive the heart of Jesus, He changes your heart. At the drop of a hat, wherever the opportunity presents itself, something as simple as a balloon becomes a witnessing tool in the huge hands of this gentle giant.

The stick and card opener

Another "opener" Blue uses is what he calls his *stick and card*. The stick is a slight-of-hand trick, or what could be called a "stick-trick" that Blue created. It is a small piece of wood in which he has drilled six holes into which he has put six jewels on each side—one side with colored jewels and the other with clear. With slight-of-hand he can make both sides look the same, or different—back and forth. As he is doing the trick he is witnessing to them.

"See, the stick is colored on both sides; now it is clear on both sides. Only Jesus can make your life clear. It's easy to fool people into thinking you're something you aren't, but you can't fool God."

He then hands the stick, which is clear on both sides, to the person he's witnessing to, and says, "How about your life? Turn it over and see." To the person's shock, the stick is no longer clear. It's multicolored, representing the person's sin. Blue then hands him or her a card on which is written:

GET OUT OF HELL FREE

For God so loved the world that He gave His only begotten Son, that whosoever believeth in Him should not perish, but have everlasting life—John 3:16
www.duaneandirisblue.com

At this writing, Blue has given out over 11,000 of these cards.

No one has ever been able to figure the trick out. When he is asked to show how he does it, he says that a lot of Christians are like magicians—they never tell their secrets. They never tell people about Jesus, and so he's not going to tell how he does the trick.

A flatbed truck and a film

Blue remembers when Ross Hargrove came to the church and asked for volunteers to help him in his street ministry—passing out tracts, going into apartment complexes where he'd set up a movie projector on the back of his flatbed truck and showing the movie, *The Cross and the Switchblade.* "I was the first to volunteer and I soon learned how God was going to use me.

"I went knocking on apartment doors with Ross. He would have me use my voice imitations to get people's attention. I'd invite them to the movie sounding like the pirate, Long John Silver, John Wayne, a robot from outer space, Mickey Mouse, or a parrot. And they would come. Lots of them.

"I cried the first time I saw the film, *The Cross and the Switchblade* which is about the conversion of Nicky Cruz, the

New York City teenage gang member. My life had been changed by the same God who had saved Nicky Cruz. That night 41 people, out of about 250, came down to the back of the truck to receive Jesus as their Savior. I prayed with three of them. It was an awesome experience.

"I began going with Ross and other folk from the church every Friday and Saturday night to different places to witness through the movie. Though I was still working my way through *Evangelism Explosion,* I wanted to be involved right away with what God was doing in the world. I had no idea at the time that I would eventually be in fulltime ministry."

A Tribute

*Bobby Conners—pastor, New Hope Baptist Church
Pinehurst, Texas*

I'll never forget the first time I saw Blue. His hair was down almost to his waist, and his untrimmed beard was almost as long. He was a sight. He had come to the church, where I was janitor, to find out what he needed to do next, now that he had been led to the Lord in the middle of the night while talking to Iris Urrey, who would one day become his wife. Outside in the church parking lot I saw his 3-wheel motorcycle with two German shepherds sitting in van seats.

It did not take long before Blue would be baptized, would cut his beard and hair, and would become a part of our church. One Sunday, after the morning service, my wife Patsy and I invited him to eat lunch with us. After the meal Patsy threw a pillow on the couch for Blue, and one on the floor for me. She said: 'Bobby always lies on the floor for a nap on Sunday so you hit the couch and join him.'

After watching something on TV for awhile, probably a sports event, I'll never forget what Blue said. 'I always wondered what families did after church on Sunday.' It was then I realized that here was a man who had never experienced the love of a family. It was a whole new thing for him, and he immediately began surrounding himself with the love of Jesus and his new family—the family of God.

One day, when Blue came to church, as he did almost every day, I heard him call in his very loud voice, "Bobby Conners, where are you?" I was in the back of the church cleaning one of the restrooms. I called back and in a moment he rushed in, all excited. He had been listening to the Bible on cassette and had heard Matthew 18:19 (KJV) read, which says, *"If two of you shall agree on earth as touching any thing that they shall ask, it shall be done for them of my Father which is in heaven."*

"That's true, isn't it Bobby?"

"Yes," I said.

"Glory to God, brother," he replied. "Me and you are going to agree that the devil is banished from earth. We are going to ask God to get rid of him right now."

I said, "Blue, we need to have a talk."

Mentoring an eager learner

When I was asked by the pastor to teach *Evangelism Explosion* at Central Baptist, Blue jumped right into the middle of it. Week after week he studied as best he could, he prayed and was faithful in attending every training session.

When the time came to practice what we had been learning, Blue, another team member and I went to a laundromat in Tomball where we encountered a young man washing his clothes. When we asked him the two questions designed to help determine his spiritual condition, we could tell by his response that he didn't know God. Blue began sharing the saving knowledge of the Lord Jesus, and when he had finished he asked the young man, "Does this make sense to you?"

"Yes," was his reply.

"Would you like to receive the Lord Jesus into your life as your Lord and Master?"

"Yes," he said again.

Blue was totally astonished. He quickly asked, "Kid, are you sure you understand what I've said?"

"Yes, I do," was his response. "I want Christ."

Blue said, "Do you realize that you have to…?"

I leaned over and whispered in Blue's ear, "Go ahead and offer to pray with him." Blue did. The young man professed the Lord Jesus right there. Blue then gave him some helpful information on walking daily with Christ and how he needed to make a public profession of his faith through baptism.

Forever friends

From those days to this, Blue and I have not only remained friends, but is has been my privilege, and the joy of New Hope Baptist Church, to follow and encourage his and Iris' ministry.

10

Family!

"God sets the lonely in families..." (Psalm 68:6 NIV).

Many of us take for granted being part of a family unit made up of parents, and perhaps a sibling or two. There are, of course, occasions when circumstances dictate a different setting, when one parent is left with the charge of rearing a family. And then, for many of us, there is the support of grandparents, uncles, aunts, or the extended family of friends and a caring church.

Have you thought, however, what it would be like to have none of the above? Have you thought what it would be like to have a father who left you and your mother when you were just a child, and who went on to marry seven more women, destroying the lives of each one? Have you thought what it would be like to have no normal home life whatsoever? Have you thought of what it would be like to have absolutely no healthy life-models to pattern yourself after, to have no one to look up to, no one to trust, no one to believe in? Nobody!

Blue's old world

This is the world into which Duane Blue was born, and it was the world he lived in for his first 33 years. This was the only world he knew. This is a world in which millions live today.

For Blue, the thought of *family* meant, at best, acquaintances he associated with in the drug and alcohol world. In the drug world, if he was to survive, he had to "get them" before they "got him." In the alcohol world, these friendships ended when he got sober.

For Blue, the word *father* created nothing but bitter memories of his own father. And when he thought of a *mother*, he was overwhelmed with sorrow and guilt, at the thought of what happened to his own mother. Such was Blue's old world.

No longer alone

But his world was beginning to change. Even before Iris left on her extended four-month trip around the world, Blue had begun to experience something that he had not known in his 33 years. He was beginning to understand what it was like to be part of a family. He was now a member of the *family of God, the body of Christ.* He had never had friends whom he could trust with his life. He had never had anyone love him, just as he was. This was, as he would put it, "blowing his mind."

And there was also another family that Blue was learning to be a part of. The Christmas experience he had with the Urreys, and the subsequent contacts they had with him, were beginning to fill another void in his life that had been there since childhood. Little things in life were taking on new meaning. Past hurts were beginning to heal, such as the crushing emotions he had experienced for years on every Mother's Day.

Mother's Day

"I hated Mother's Day. It was the worst day of the year for me. All it did was bring back memories of my own mother's suicide that I blamed on myself. But now, even Mother's Day was beginning to have new meaning."

With Iris on the other side of the world, Blue went to the florist and purchased a dozen long-stemmed roses, climbed on his 3-wheeler, and with his dogs, headed for Outlaw Bend. He knew what to expect when he knocked on the door. He would again find himself in the embrace of a woman who had loved him when he was so unlovable.

"Granny," he said (everybody called her Granny), "I have never liked Mother's Day but because you have opened your heart and home to me, I've brought these roses to express my love and thanks for all you've done for me."

She said: "Keep calling me Granny, but I'll be your mother for this Mother's Day." Then came the hug that seemed to never let go. They asked him to spend the whole day with them.

"I ate with them. I talked with them. Pat Urrey, Iris's dad, treated me like a son. He told me what was going on in his life. He sat there and listened to me. What an incredible family.

"As I drove the two hours back to my bus that night, it began to really register that I was actually a new person, and that I was now being treated like family by these folks, though at that point I never dreamed that one day I would marry their daughter."

11

Romance in the Air

When Iris left on her around-the-world ministry trip with a group that included Jack Taylor and Glenn Sheppard, she left Blue with a couple of contact addresses. Knowing, however, how difficult it would be for him to write, she did not expect to hear from him, so it was to her surprise that a letter was waiting for her in South Korea and another in Germany. Though it took a good bit of deciphering to understand what he'd written, she was finally able to get the gist of what he was trying to say.

II Hesitations 2:5

In the midst of all that was happening in his life, Blue was now finding himself looking forward more and more to Iris' return home. Something actually was stirring in both their hearts, and it would not be long after Iris' return that they would begin to sense that God intended their relationship to be more than friendship.

When she did finally return, she told Blue that it was the first time she had seen him clothed, shaved, and in his right mind. She was referring to his having shaved off his beard and cut his hair.

Iris introduced Blue to tithing. He thought that was the coolest thing! He was so excited at the thought of giving something to God. He told her that he was going to give God more than that. She said: "Have you paid your rent yet?"

"No, but that's not due for another ten days."

Iris said: "Just remember, if you give God what belongs to your landlord He's going to bless your landlord, not you."

As interesting an interpretation as this was, it did help Blue understand that, though the tithe goes to God first, God doesn't want money that belongs to other people. After the tithe, they get paid, then from what is left decide how much more you are going to give to Him.

Iris invited Blue to join her in Atlanta for a speaking engagement sponsored by Truett Cathy, founder and CEO of Chick-fil-A. Blue flew to Atlanta where he enjoyed being "wined and dined" by Mr. Cathy. It was a special time that would turn out to be but the first of other occasions when he and Iris would meet, and it was not long before they began seeing each other in a different light.

One day, when in a lighter mood, Iris told Blue that she had read in *II Hesitations 2:5* that if he didn't marry the person who led him to the Lord he was in danger of losing his salvation.

Will you?

One autumn evening, while eating at *The Dragon Inn* in Tomball, Texas, Blue knelt down and asked Iris to be his bride. When Iris responded to his "Will you?" with her "I will," Blue went on to lay down three conditions that would need to be met if they were to marry.

"Iris, I don't want to do anything that will hurt your ministry because God is using you in a great way. I don't think God is going to use me the same way He is using you, so, if you agree, I'll go back into construction and will support and encourage you in everything God has for you.

"The second condition is that you speak to the men on your board and get their OK, and the third, I'll go home and ask my pastor, Billy Crosby, what he thinks about our getting married."

This may seem a bit unconventional and backward, but very little in the lives of these special servants of God has been, or is, conventional. Receiving affirmation from everyone they talked to, all they now had to do was decide on the when and where of the wedding.

Foiled plans

When they settled on a February date at First Baptist Church, Euless, Texas, Marthé Beasley and friends began plotting and planning. It was going to be quite an affair. Six ministers were going to participate, beginning with brother Manley—that is, until a December prison crusade, where Iris was to have spoken, was cancelled due to a prison riot. With this date opening up on the calendar, and with a growing concern on their part that the wedding being planned was going to cost a lot more than they were comfortable with, Blue and Iris decided to get married that next weekend in the little country church in Votaw, Texas, where Iris' parents were members.

There was, however, one problem—how were they going to break the news to those who were planning the big affair in February? They called Manley Beasley.

With his counsel and blessing, they decided not to say anything to anyone who was working on the other date until after the fact, so arrangements were quickly made with the bi-vocational pastor of *Votaw Baptist Church* near Outlaw Bend.

December 9, 1984

The plan was for Blue and Iris to be in attendance at the morning worship service, then, immediately following the closing prayer, the pastor would invite the wedding party to step forward. As they did, the flower arrangement on the pulpit table would be exchanged for a wedding bouquet, and all of this, of course, would be to the surprise of everyone in attendance, except for Iris' parents. This would be a day of double blessing for the Urreys—their daughter's wedding and Mirrell's birthday.

Blue still carries several special memories with him from that day. The pastor, who had broken one of the lenses in his glasses that morning, inserted a lens from his prescription sunglasses. He performed the ceremony with one dark and one clear eye.

For the reception, a lady in the church baked a beautiful three-tier wedding cake at the last minute, as well as a chocolate groom's cake for Blue. The reception had to be brief because Blue and Iris needed to catch a 6:30 PM flight from Houston's Hobby Airport to Dallas because Iris had agreed to give her testimony in a Fort Worth church where Bro. Manley was preaching.

Meeting Marthé

They were surprised to be met at the airport by Marthé Beasley, and though she was still upset at the change in wedding plans that she had only heard about the day before, she entertained them all the way to the church in Fort Worth.

The service was well under way when they arrived, but when Manley saw them walk in, he stopped everything to introduce the congregation to Mr. and Mrs. Duane Blue. The entire church stood and applauded. As they clapped, it began to dawn on Blue—the reality of what had happened in a short nine months was beginning to register. He was now, not only a believer, but married to the one whom God had used to lead him to faith. This was the beginning of the rest of his life. The night was young and there were surprises yet to come.

Following the service Manley, Marthé and their four children took Blue and Iris out to a restaurant to celebrate their nuptials after which Marthé, the chauffeur, drove them back to the airport to retrieve their luggage before being taken to their hotel. Surprise: The baggage-claim office had closed, so they had to wait until the next day to retrieve their belongings.

Next morning—7:30 AM

Knock, knock, knock. "Hello, hello, hello. This is Marthé Ann. I've come to take you to the mall. We're going to shop for some new outfits before you drive to Georgia. I'll be waiting."

Scramble... scramble... They shopped 'til noon, an experience Blue remembers to this day. He had never been led by the hand from one store to the next, and never in his life had he tried on as many outfits as he did that day. Finally, after the shopping, luggage retrieval, and car rental, Blue and Iris, barely married for 24 hours, headed toward Georgia and the next "assignment!" Iris was scheduled to speak to 720 women in a maximum security prison the next day. And what an experience that was.

"There were all kinds of brokenness and weeping. I heard Iris talking in a prison slang language that I could hardly understand. She was using words that only hardened criminals understood. I'd been in jail lots of times, in the north and the south, for robbery, drugs, and stuff, but the longest I'd spent behind bars was 90 days. So I hadn't picked up a lot of that vocabulary."

Back to Texas

When Blue and Iris finished their "prison honeymoon," they headed back to Texas where they bought a little house trailer and set it up in Magnolia. Iris was traveling a lot and Blue returned to painting and construction. He had decided to do it for free, just like he had done before they were married, and to trust God to meet their needs. He just wanted to help people.

With that commitment, it would not be long before Blue began to see some incredible things happen. One day when he was painting a house, a neighbor came over and put $200 in his hand. Another man, who saw the sign that said he was working for Jesus, gave him a whole set of tools. That kind of thing was happening day after day. "I was blown away," remembers Blue.

Sometimes when Iris had a meeting within driving distance Blue would go with her, and a few times he even flew to a meeting. On one of these occasions, Iris spoke at a church where Ronnie Yarborough was pastor.

"She spoke that evening," recalls Blue. "And it was an awesome meeting. Then, out of nowhere, I heard the pastor say, 'I know it's late, but how many of you would like to hear Blue give his testimony?'

"I couldn't believe what I was hearing. 'No way,' I said. 'Not me. I've never done that before.'

"Ronnie said, 'Come on Blue. Take about 15 to 20 minutes. We want to hear your testimony.'

"I was terrified," recalls Blue. "But I couldn't get out of it, so I got up, and spoke for what seemed an hour and a half. It was only for eight minutes. But what blew my mind was that a man got saved when I finished."

More doors open…but?

Though Blue began getting more invitations to share his testimony he was getting suspicious that it was because he was married to Iris. Because of that he decided he would stay home and serve people through his work, help around the church, and touch people's lives by just talking to them about Jesus.

Then one day, while he was sitting at home by himself, the phone rang. It was George Harris, a pastor in San Antonio. Blue told him that Iris had gone to North Carolina for a meeting but that he would have her call him when she got home. Dr. Harris said: "Blue, I didn't phone to speak to Iris; I'm calling to talk to you. A friend of mine had you share your testimony and I would like you to come and speak at my church."

"I don't do that," replied Blue.

"Yes you do," he said. "I'm sending you a plane ticket and I expect to see you here Sunday morning."

"It freaked me out, but I flew to San Antonio," recalls Blue. "They put me up in a motel and I shared my testimony in the Sunday morning service. I was blown away."

A few weeks later Blue got a call from Tommy Gilmore who was a ministry associate of Dr. Charles Stanley at First Baptist Church in Atlanta. He said: "Dr. Stanley wants you to come and speak on Sunday night."

"They flew me to Atlanta, picked me up, took me to a hotel and I spoke that night," remembers Blue. "God blessed. People were saved. I was blown away. I knew that I didn't want people to expect that I'd be in the ministry because I was married to Iris, but this seemed to be different."

Blue was then asked by Carlos McLeod to take a few minutes to share his testimony at the Texas Evangelism Conference.

"That was one of the most powerful moments of my life. But I was beginning to be torn. I had thought I would be supporting Iris by working in construction and painting, but now, I began to wonder if God wanted to actually use me in a speaking ministry. I had to find out. I was going to have to decide. I was going to have to hear from God if He wanted me in fulltime ministry. I felt that if He did, I was going to have to go all the way. But, how am I going to know?"

Blue asked tons of people. He asked Ron Dunn. He asked Bro. Manley. He asked this one and that one, and he would always get the same answer, "You'll just know. If God's in it, you'll know." But how?

God's time is not always our time. It would not be until Blue and Iris had moved to Europe for a year and would make a trip into a communist country to meet one of God's choice couples, that Blue would finally know, beyond any doubt, what God's plan was for his life.

12

When Two Become One

Some people think the answer is to marry
the greatest person they have ever met;
But what a rude awakening to discover
the one they marry isn't perfect yet.
It doesn't take too long before they're finding
that marriage is much more than having fun.
When two are joined as one in matrimony
life's learning times have only just begun.[14]

Though they knew it would not be easy, in light of their each being such strong personalities, along with the amount of baggage each carried into the union, Blue and Iris could never have anticipated just how difficult marriage was initially going to be. Looking at it strictly from the world's perspective, this marriage was doomed to fail from the beginning. By God's grace, however, and with the prayer support and counsel of those who dearly loved them, they would persevere, in spite of those moments when they themselves wondered if they would ever make it.

And thrown into the mix was the overtime effort the enemy was going to exert to destroy what he knew were two special trophies of God's grace. He used every scheme he could to defeat them, and there were times when he almost succeeded. One of those occasions took place less than a year into the marriage. They were at a point of calling it quits. Blue looks back.

---

[14] From the song, *When Two Become One*. Words by Ron Owens.

Sandpaper and a grinder

"We were living in a trailer in Magnolia, Texas. We had just had another big fight and as far as I was concerned I was ready to quit, and I knew Iris felt the same way. Bro. Manley Beasley was in a meeting less than an hour away, and since he had so much to do with our getting married in the first place, I thought it was only fair to phone him to tell him that we were probably going to get a divorce. He told me that he would drive over right after the meeting that night.

"When I told Iris he was coming, she hit the ceiling. She got madder than ever because she respected Bro. Manley so much and she didn't want to disappoint him. When he arrived she was still mad. As he walked through the door she said: 'Well, have you come to referee?'

"'No, sister,' he said. 'I've come to take over. You sit down and listen. Both of you.'

"I'll never forget what he told us. It was short and to the point.

"'You two can just pull down those shades and live for Satan and be of no value to each other or to the Kingdom of God, or you can get right with God and with each other, and go on to be of some value to Him. Blue, walk me to the car. I'm going back to my motel.'

"I thought, 'Is that all he's going to do? That ain't going to help.' Well, he did have more to say when we got outside. 'Blue, if there's one thing that you are going to have to learn about marriage, it's this. Your mate is your heavenly sandpaper, but son, you've got a grinder.'

"I couldn't believe what I heard. I got mad at him because I thought he was insulting Iris. I began to defend her, that is until he hit me with, 'In your case, Blue, sandpaper would never do the job. You needed a grinder and He gave you one.' With that, he drove off, but what Bro. Manley taught us that night has seen us through many rough waters since then, and God is still grinding away."

As iron sharpens iron, and as God's grace was being poured into their lives, Blue and Iris continued growing in their walk with the Lord, and in their walk with each other.

A new church home

Not too long after this marriage crisis, Carlos McLeod, Director of Evangelism for the Texas Baptist Convention, invited the Blues to give their testimonies at Robinwood Baptist Church in Seagoville, where he was preaching in a revival. Little did Blue and Iris realize the significant role this meeting would play in their future. A relationship would be forged with a pastor that lasts to this day, and it would be in the Seagoville Church that their son, Denim, would one day be surrounded and loved by Robinwood's extended family.

Sunday morning eye-opener

"Iris, can you believe what we just saw? I didn't know there were churches like this. I think we need to be here."

"Well, what's keeping us from moving to Seagoville?"

"Nothing, I guess, except that we're going to fly to Europe next week and we'll be there for a year."

"We've got a week."

What Blue and Iris had experienced in that morning service was a bit out-of-the-ordinary. A man had gone to the altar at the end of the service expressing his desire to receive Christ as his Savior. After being counseled, he shared with the pastor that his wife had recently died, that he had two little girls to care for, and that he had just lost his job. Pastor Jim Everidge then turned to the congregation, explained the situation and asked:

"What do you think we should do?"

A man jumped to his feet and said: "I'll give him a job."

"No way," called out another. "You gave the last person a job. It's my turn."

Two ladies then stood to say that they would arrange to have evening meals prepared for him, and that they would provide childcare for his two little girls every weekday.

This was the kind of church the Blues had dreamed about but didn't know existed, but if they were going to be a part of this church they were going to have to move quickly as they were about to fly to Europe where they would be ministering for the next 12 months. They decided that they only had time to move their membership, so after hauling their trailer and the two German shepherds up to Iris' parents' farm near Rye, and just a few days before they flew to Brussels, Belgium, they joined Robinwood Baptist Church in Seagoville, Texas.

No casual relationship

Their relationship to a church body has always been fundamentally important to Blue and Iris. They have never been just casual members, but have poured themselves into the life and work of whatever church they were part of. In a day when many itinerate ministers are church members in name only, Iris and Blue can be found right in the middle of whatever is going on in their church family—giving and serving. Interestingly, while they were in Europe, they tithed to both their home church in Seagoville and to the International Baptist Church in Brussels, their home-away-from-home that year.

A Tribute

Jim Everidge—pastor of Cornerstone Baptist Church
Lucas, Texas

Up until their move to Athens, Texas, in 2010, Jim Everidge had been the Blue's pastor on three occasions—Robinwood Baptist Church in Seagoville, Texas, First Baptist in Sachet and Cornerstone Baptist in Lucas. In addition to being their pastor, he has been a close friend and encourager through the years.

I once preached a message titled, *The Gospel According to the Blues,* on a Sunday when they were not present. I used Acts 4:13 (KJV) that talks about what Annas, the High Priest, Caiaphas, and others observed when Peter and John stood before them. They *"marveled and took knowledge of them, that they had been with Jesus."*

Something I have observed during the years I have known the Blues is that when you have truly been with Jesus you are going to have a *lop-sided lifestyle*—your life will be totally dedicated to living for Jesus.

When you are with the Blues you also soon discover that they have a *limited vocabulary*—all they want to talk about is Jesus. Oh, how we need more of their kind in our churches today.

Duane and Iris' faith is contagious. When they were saved they didn't meet a church, they met a living Lord. The *source, supply and song* of their lives and ministry has been Jesus. That's what blesses me when I think of them. You can't say that about a lot of people who belong to our churches today.

My verse for the Blues as a family is 2 Corinthians 5:17 (KJV): *"Therefore, if any man be in Christ, he is a new creature..."* If people don't believe that God can make a change in a person's life, they have never met Duane and Iris Blue. Talk is cheap in America, and sadly, that is also true in the church—from the pulpit to the pew. The thing about Duane, and his wife/ministry partner, Iris, is what you see is what you get.

Section Three

Going International

We've a story to tell to the nations
That shall turn their hearts to the right,
A story of truth and mercy,
A story of peace and light.

We've a song to be sung to the nations
That shall lift their hearts to the Lord,
A song that shall conquer evil
And shatter the spear and sword.[15]

---

[15] Words by H. Ernest Nichol

13

Europe

Though Iris had already travelled abroad on many occasions, this was the first time Blue had ever been beyond the borders of the United States.

They had been invited by the *European Baptist Convention* to spend a year ministering on the continent in EBC churches, as well as with the US military, particularly in NATO schools.

God's provision begins

When the owner of *North American Van Lines* heard that Blue and Iris were heading to Europe for a year, he offered to ship free anything they wanted to take with them, and anything they would want to bring back to the States. He sent a container to their home where Blue loaded his construction and painting tools, including a hydraulic paint rig, air compressor, nail gun, cases of nails, and a variety of saws. All this, plus everything else they were going to need to set up housekeeping, was shipped, six weeks prior to their own departure, to Antwerp, Holland.

When the container arrived, Colonel Dan Buttolph, who had gotten to know Iris on her previous trips to Europe, and who, along with his wife, Shay, had been instrumental in opening up the doors to the NATO schools, provided Blue a special power-conversion unit that the military uses to transform electric currency from 240 volts down to 120. This unit also served for cycle conversion, which was important in the operation of certain tools.

God's abundant provision continues

God had already gone ahead of them by not only preparing the way for their ministry, but also in arranging for their housing needs. Think of this…

When they boarded their plane in Dallas, Blue and Iris were leaving behind his old bus, which they had driven up to Iris' parents' farm in Outlaw Bend, Texas, along with the two German shepherds.[16] When they set foot on European soil, they moved into a beautiful three-bedroom house provided by members of the Brussels *International Baptist Church* who would be out of the country for most of the time Iris and Blue were to be in Europe.

But that wasn't all that God was providing. Along with this beautiful home came the use of two automobiles, fish delivered to the door every Thursday, and milk every other day!! When the owners returned, the Blues were asked to "house-sit" a lovely 10th-story apartment in downtown Brussels for a church member who also had to travel abroad.

Ministry begins

This would be a year of travelling from country to country, ministering in churches and schools, and when home, being involved in the ministry of the *International Baptist Church*, where Phil Roberts was pastor.

Blue had been asked by the Brussels church to help in the reconstruction of a building they had purchased, however, due to a nine-month delay in acquiring the necessary permits, he was not able to assist them with this particular project.

But that did not stop him from using his construction and painting skills in other places of need. When he was not on the road with Iris, he was fixing things up around the Brussels IBC, and when time permitted, he was out helping with the facility

---

[16] They had given their house trailer to a lady who simply had to pick up the payments.

needs of other churches in the convention. He painted the Permisan Church inside and out, and worked on the Emmanuel Baptist Church building in Hoensbroek, The Netherlands, where their friend, Larry Carson, was pastor.

During 10 days when they were headquartered at the Baptist Seminary in Ruschlikon, Switzerland, he repaired desks, among other things. He raised a ruckus, however, when he suggested they tear the heavy quarter-inch copper gutters off the roofs, along with the down-spouts, and sell the copper for at least several hundred thousand dollars that could have been invested in missions! This was not too well received by the seminary leadership.

A NATO high school assembly

During Iris' previous times in Europe, NATO schools across Europe had opened up to her ministry, and now that she was married these doors were still there for them to walk through. And through them they went.

When doing the NATO school assemblies they would often use the "two cakes" illustration[17] to show where rebellion can lead. When Iris gets to the point where she pulls out the jalapeno peppers and dumps them into her cake mix, she says: "You know, you should have sex out of marriage. Why not? That's hot stuff."

At one of these NATO school assemblies, as she was walking up to the stage, Iris overheard two boys chuckling: "What do those fat people know about drugs?"

She stopped, looked at them, and said: "If you will listen, these two fat people have got something to say to you." The expressions on the boys faces looked like somebody had sucked all the air out of the room.

While this was going on, Blue noticed another kid messing around with a girl sitting beside him. Blue walked over to them, and looking at the girl, said:

---

[17] See Chapter 18, *A Tale of Two Cakes*

"Man, I really like that purple thing on the side of your neck. I'd like to get something like that to put on my wife's neck."

She proudly said, "My man put it there."

"Really? What man?" replied Blue, in a tone indicating his surprise that she would call the little punk sitting beside her a man.

"Wait around after we bake the two cakes. I want to see what you think." Then to Blue's surprise, the girl, seeming to anticipate what was going to happen, not only repeated about her "man" putting that tattoo on her neck, but volunteered that she only had sex with guys she loved. Blue knew at that point that the kid sitting next to her hadn't been her only "man."

Later

At the end of the cake demonstration, during which the boy was giving Blue dirty looks, and the young girl was visibly agitated, the "man," attempting to show his "manhood," volunteered to eat Iris' cake. So, up he came.

Blue, however, sensitive to what was going on between this kid and the girl, decided to approach the situation from a different angle.

"Young man, let's pretend that these aren't cakes. Let's pretend that these are women. Let's pretend that you have a great job, lots of money, and you have a new Porsche…"

The boy interrupted; "A red one!"

"OK," said Blue, "a red one. Now," looking at the cakes, "we're pretending these two cakes are women. Which one do you want to be your wife? How about Iris' cake?"

"That's stupid," said the kid. "No way! Nobody would want that one. It's a bunch of trash."

At that point, the little girl, who could see where Blue was heading, began to cry. Interestingly, not only did the two young people know what was going on between them, but the teachers and the rest of the school knew as well. God was in the process of dealing with a growing problem in the NATO schools, an issue that is almost everywhere in our schools today.

When the assembly was over, Blue and Iris headed straight for those young people. They knew they needed to have some one-on-one time with them, which resulted in the young lady asking God to forgive her and praying to receive the Lord Jesus as her Savior. The smart-aleck boy, however, turned out to be just that—*an obnoxiously conceited and self-assertive person with pretensions of smartness...*[18] He walked away.

A lesson learned—the hard way

"You have heard that it was said, 'You shall love your neighbor and hate your enemy.' But I say to you, love your enemies...and pray for those who...persecute you..." (Matthew 5:43-44, NKJV)

"Because Ron Owens could speak both French and English," recalls Blue, "several *Rock* radio stations in Brussels, Belgium, had asked Ron to record a series of two-hour programs that they would air in the evening, once a week, for the *International Community*. They said he could play Christian music and say whatever he wanted to, all he had to do was play music that had "the sound" of their stations. This seemed like a good witnessing opportunity so he agreed to do it.

"That was during the time me and Iris were living in Europe, and because the home that we had been given to live in had plenty of room, we invited Ron to stay with us.

"I started going with him to some of the recording sessions and was beginning to get upset. No, not just upset, I was getting mad at what the recording engineers were doing! Sometimes, if they didn't like what Ron was saying, they would cut him off, or they would start playing music right over his voice. They were doing all kinds of things to make it difficult for him.

---

[18] Definition from the Merriam Webster dictionary

"I had only been saved for a little more than a year and was still struggling with how to do stuff, with how to respond to frustrating situations in a different way than I used to. So, after about three days of watching what they were doing I began to lose it. I told Ron that, if he wanted me to, I would take care of those guys in the control room. I could fix it so that they'd never do it again. I told him that the next time they cut him off I would slam them against the wall. And I could have done it because I was bigger than the two of them put together.

"That's when I saw a situation being handled in a totally different way than I was accustomed to seeing. I witnessed the difference between *wisdom* and *foolishness*. I was blown away, and it blew those two radio engineer guys away too. Instead of dealing with it 'my way,' Ron said: 'No, Blue, I'm going to give them $100 this morning.'

"What? They're jerks, man. After what they've been doing to you?

'Yeah, I don't like them either, so I need to invest in them. The Bible says that 'where your treasure is there will your heart be also.' My heart's not with them and I need to have it there. I need to invest some love into them. They know we are Christians and no telling how the Lord will use this investment.'

"That was one of the most amazing learning events in my life. It is something that I've tried to practice ever since— giving, even when someone doesn't deserve it; giving without expecting to get anything back. If we had done it *my way,* I would have felt good for a moment, but it sure would have messed up our witness."

Author's note: And both of us would have been thrown in jail and would have become an international incident.

14

The Call

Zilina, Czechoslovakia, 1986

The highlight of that year in Europe was a trip Blue and Iris made to Zilina, Czechoslovakia, to visit Vlado and Ruth Fajfr. Czechoslovakia was still under communism in 1986 and this was the first visit Blue had made to that part of the world, though Iris had been there on several occasions. Zilina was a city in the Slovak part of Czechoslovakia that is now the country of Slovakia.

Ruth had been the wife and ministry partner of James Alexander Stewart but had been widowed for a number of years when the Lord brought Vlado back into her life. He had come to faith in Christ years before in the city of Brno when she and James were ministering there. He had become one of Czechoslovakia's outstanding sportsmen and had also earned his doctor of law degree. What set him apart from many of his peers, however, was his total commitment to be an unashamed witness for Christ, right in the middle of a communist country.

The authorities could not silence him, though they tried with many imprisonments. When they could not shut Vlado up, they moved him and his family about as far away from Prague as they could, to the eastern region of the country, where it was not long before he started a church. The severe persecution that the family was put through, however, resulted in the untimely death of his first wife.

A first impression

Blue had heard a lot about the Fajfrs from Iris, and he was looking forward to meeting this godly couple. Blue will never forget what happened when they stepped onto the train platform and were met by the Fajfrs.

After the embraces and greetings, Vlado said, "Please wait for just a moment. I need to talk to these people over here about Jesus." He explained later what he had said. Since sports was such an important part of his early life, he sometimes used a sports' analogy in his witness.

"Dobrey den (Good day). I would like to tell you a story about a football match that is found in the book of John in the Bible. One team was made up of Jesus and His boys, and the other team was made up of the Sadducees and Pharisees. The Sadducees and the Pharisees know all the rules but play by none of them. Jesus and his boys don't know the rules but they are for fair play. Which team would you like to be on? Look up those two teams in the book of John in the Bible. Read about them and decide which team you want to be on."

"Valdo," recalls Blue, "was the most impressive and creative witness I have ever known."

Getting an answer

Blue had not been saved long when he arrived on the European continent, and he was still not sure what God intended for his life. When he told Vlado that he was struggling with whether he should be in the ministry full time or whether he should keep working in construction and help support Iris in her ministry, he didn't expect what happened next.

"Well, my brother," said Vlado. "Let me tell you. We must go to the Lord for this. I go now to my bedroom and kneel at foot of bed and pray for you. You now go to your room and open God's Word while I spend time on my face until God gives you answer from His Word. Go to room. Go! Open God's Word. You will have confirmation if He wants you for fulltime work or to work in the world and to serve Jesus with the people. Find your word."

Blue thought, "Huh? Did he say he was going to go to his bedroom and stay on his face, praying for me until I get an answer? Either this man is crazy or God is speaking to him."

As Blue walked upstairs he was struggling. "God, where do I even start? Where in the Bible do I go? I still don't read very well." He got his Bible, and being the young Christian he was, popped it open and put his finger down. He looked to see where he was and discovered that he had put his finger on verse 13 of 1 Timothy 4: "Until I come, devote yourself to the public reading of Scripture, to preaching and teaching."

"I went, 'Wow! Until Jesus comes?' Blue recalls. "I couldn't believe what had happened. I went downstairs, weeping. I said, 'Mr. Fajfr, I know what I'm supposed to do until Jesus comes back. I'm to give my life to reading, preaching, and teaching the Scriptures. I'm to tell people about what Jesus has done for me. Thank you sir, for helping me.'

"That day in the Fajfr home in Zilina, Czechoslovakia, will always be marked in my mind. It was the day I knew that I was to spend the rest of my life telling people about Jesus."

A most precious gift

There were more wonderful teaching moments for Blue during this time with the Fajfrs. He went with Vlado to witness in prisons, schools, homes, and all kinds of places. It was the first time he had the experience of sharing his testimony through an interpreter.

Then after breakfast on the fourth day of that first visit, Vlado asked Blue to join him in the music room. He sat at the piano and played for a few minutes[19] while Iris and Ruth stayed in the kitchen. Suddenly he stopped, turned to Blue and said:

---

[19] Vlado was an accomplished musician who played for Ruth every morning as she was preparing herself for the day.

"Brother Blue, I would like to ask you a question. Do you love your wife?"

"I was floored," recalls Blue. "'Yes, of course I do,' was my reply. He said: 'Maybe you are a bit untruthful with me, yes?' I was like, 'What?' Vlado continued.

"'I need you to understand something. I lost my first wife under communism. She suffered so because of what they were doing to me. Then, when God gave me Miss Ruth, I made a promise that not a day would go by that I wouldn't be God's mouth in her presence—not a day would pass when we would not read Scripture together and pray together. I would like to give you a book that we read together every morning and every night.'"

The Daily Light[20]

At that, he retrieved a copy of the devotional, *The Daily Light,* from the bookshelf and handed it to Blue, saying:

"I will promise you that every morning and evening I will read these words to my Duckie[21] and I want to ask you if you will do the same with your Iris; if you will read to her and pray with her every morning and every night."

"That was in 1986," recalls Blue, "and to this day we are still reading *The Daily Light* and praying together.

"I believe this is one of the main reasons me and Iris have stayed together, even when we wanted to kill each other. When

---

[20] For over a century, *Daily Light on the Daily Path* has been a favorite devotional book of those who realize the tremendous benefit of reading and praying Scripture. Originally printed in the mid-1800s, *Daily Light* was born out of the devout faith of Samuel Bagster, a British bookstore owner determined to share his faith with his 12 children. The Bagsters' daily practice of reading Scripture together, then connecting the day's verses with other passages, inspired one of the children to compile their devotions for publication.

[21] Vlado's term of endearment for his wife.

Denim came along he became a part of the family reading and prayer time. Every day we read, I am reminded where it all started—in the music room of Vlado and Ruth Fajfr's home in Zilina, Czechoslovakia, in 1986 when he asked me the question, 'Do you love your wife?'

"We carry a picture of Vlado and Ruth in the *The Daily Light* devotional, and every day, when we look at it, we thank God for loving us enough to bring the Fajfrs into our lives. Learning to read and pray together has been one of the greatest gifts God has given to our marriage. I will always be in their debt."

Through the years Iris and Blue returned to visit the Fajfrs nine times, almost until they both went home to be with the Lord.

A Tribute

David Nix, Ph.D.—Missionary to Indonesia
Australian Baptist Convention

I'm feeling a little nervous, as well as excited, as I ride the elevator to the 18th floor of the *Hyde Park Plaza Hotel* in downtown Sydney.

It is March 1987, and several days have passed since I returned home to Australia after spending 15 months ministering in India where I had become used to living in a socially conservative setting among missionaries.

My parents, Norm and Marjory Nix, have told me about a godly missionary couple who, just a few days earlier, had arrived from Texas. Now I was about to meet them. "What will they be like?" I ask myself. "Will they sit me down and share some deep spiritual truth? Will they pray a blessing over me? Will they ask me about how my devotional life is going?"

I knock on the door of their hotel room. A deep, very loud voice yells, "Come on in, it's not locked." I open the door and am confronted by this giant of a man. He orders me to follow him to the balcony. I think, "Is he going to throw me over the railing?"

"Pick up that water balloon," he orders, "and hand it to me. Quick!" The only option I see is to do what he says. Out of the corner of my eye I notice a sling-shot contraption attached to the balcony railing. With huge arms and massive chest, this Grizzly Adams-looking man attaches the water balloon to the sling and pulls back as far as he can. He takes aim, and lets go. The water balloon goes sailing through the air, across a road intersection, and explodes at street level, 18 floors below, right in the middle of a group of punk-rockers. "Alright," he roars in boyish delight. "Got 'em!" He then extends his meaty hand to me. "You can call me Blue!" he says.

Over the succeeding years I have been blessed to spend significant periods of time with Blue. Significant, because I have learned much from him, as Jesus has used him to help shape my life. I have learned much about faith and generosity from Blue as I have watched him bless others while trusting the Lord Jesus to provide for his own family. I have witnessed Blue's love for the Word of God and his diligence in reading and studying it. Interestingly, in the early years I knew him, he could barely read at all, but he has persevered and his devotion to God's Word has continued to grow. I have also seen Blue mature as a husband and father. He is a man who cares deeply for his family.

The one thing that stands out most to me, however, is his love for Jesus and his deep gratitude for what the Lord Jesus has done in his life. Because of this joy and amazement over what God has done in setting him free from the perverted life of drugs and all that world involved, he longs for others to experience this same joy and freedom. He longs for those who are bound by the same chains that bound him for years to be made clean and fresh and be given a new start in life.

I have often seen Blue weep as he shares with others about Jesus' love—in churches, restaurants, football games, high schools, colleges, and prisons. My prayer for myself, and everyone who reads this book, is that we'll have a similar passion for those who are without the Savior. Blue continues to be that kind of inspiration and blessing to me. His is a living testimony to the grace and saving power of the Lord Jesus.

15

Down Under and Under and Under...

A Providential encounter

Norman Nix, president of the Australian Mid-South Wales Baptist Convention, and his wife, Marjory, were invited by Texas' Southern Baptists to attend their annual Evangelism Conference in the summer of 1987. When Blue and Iris gave their testimonies, Norman knew that he was hearing something that could be powerfully used "down under," so he and Marjory prayed, right there, about inviting the Blues to Australia. But how were they going to find them in such a large crowd?

Back at their hotel the Nixes pushed the elevator button and waited. The door opened and there stood Blue and Iris. "We've just been praying about inviting you to come to Australia and here you are. Do you think you could come for three months?" asked Norm.

It would not take long for the details to be worked out between Texas Baptists and the Mid-South Wales Convention for Blue and Iris to go to Australia. A partnership had just been established between the Texas and Australian conventions, and Carlos McLeod, the Texas Baptist Evangelism Director, was excited to have his friends, Blue and Iris, be the first Texas envoys sent to the southern hemisphere under this cooperative endeavor.

An open door

And so, Blue and Iris embarked on one of the most exciting ministry adventures of their lives. When they arrived, it was evident that the Lord had already been preparing the way. One of the more significant ministries that immediately began to open up was being invited to speak in Australian school assemblies. They were permitted to share their testimony without restrictions being put on them and, in most schools, they were even permitted to extend an invitation to receive Christ.

Their uniqueness was not lost on Australian media either, and soon they became headline material in print, radio, and television. They were considered celebrities. Television crews followed them to school assemblies and filmed their lectures on where rebellion and drugs can lead. What they shared in one city was played in its entirety on the evening TV news.

Come to my office

Following one of these assemblies, during their third time in Australia, a school principal asked Blue to come to his office. "I need you to talk to a lad who has been in a lot of trouble," he said. "We had to kick him out of school last year and have him institutionalized because he threatened a teacher with a knife. We recently let him return, but he has already been busted twice. He comes from a single-parent home and he is in my office right now. He's crying. I've never seen him cry before."

Blue went to the principal's office and found a very distraught young man who had just heard Blue's testimony. He blurted out: "I don't want to end up like you did. I don't want my mother to kill herself. I'm a terrible problem to her. I steal from her all the time and I'm afraid that if I don't change, she'll die. I don't want her to die. What can I do?"

Blue recalls how what happened next seemed almost foolish, but it was at that moment that he saw something that Manley Beasley had once talked to him about. Bro. Manley had told him that every event in his life might one day be used of the Lord to help in someone else's life.

"Young man," Blue said. "You heard my testimony about me living in a bus with two German shepherd dogs who rode on the back of my motorcycle everywhere I went?"

"Yes sir," he said.

"Well, if either you or me could snap our fingers and turn one of those dogs into a man, what would he know to do? Just because he was instantly changed from being a dog into being a man doesn't mean he will know what to do as a man. What if this "man" ran out of the building with the other dog and followed him around? All he would know to do is what he sees dogs doing.

"Son, I ran with dogs most of my life, but the moment Jesus changed me I knew that I couldn't run with dogs anymore. They represented the booze and drugs and all the other junk of the world I used to be in. All that mattered to me now was that Jesus Christ had changed my life and I wanted to learn what this meant, so I spent as much time as I could in church and around other believers who would help me understand what I had become. I knew I had to stay as far away from the old world as I could, because it would try to suck me right back in.

"I didn't care what the church thought of me with my long hair and beard; I just wanted to be where Jesus was and find out what He was doing. You see, young man, you've got to give all you are to Jesus and turn away from what you've been as fast as you can so you can become what Jesus wants you to be. Does that make sense? Are you ready to turn from what you've been and give your life to Jesus?"

"Yes sir," he said. "I know what I need to do."

"Would you like me to lead you in a prayer to receive Jesus as your Savior?" asked Blue.

"No sir, I think I know what to do." He then cried out, "God, I'm a dog. I've been a dog most of my life, but I want to be a man and get away from all the things that have been in my life. I want to get with people who will teach me how to be a man."

"Though that may not have been the typical 'sinner's prayer,' I know that young boy was saved that day," recalls Blue. "I did lead him in another prayer and then introduced him to a local pastor who took this young lad under his wing.

"Brother Manley was right. God can take anything He wants from your past and use it for His glory, even something as foolish as dogs."

Ian in Australia

On an earlier trip, after an assembly in another school, some of the teenage boys who had responded to the invitation to receive Christ asked permission to meet with Blue afterward to ask questions about what had just happened. They were joined by several other teenagers who were already believers.

Ian, one of the "new converts," asked Blue what he needed to do next—what he should do with his life. Blue told him he needed to find a church home, make a public profession of his faith through baptism, and then find someone to pray with on a regular basis.

Ian surprised Blue with how quickly he picked up on the praying part.

"I'd like to start a prayer group right here at the school, but I need someone to join me and help me learn how to pray. Who can help me?"

Blue looked around the room that was full of kids, many who said they were Christians, but not one of them volunteered until finally one boy spoke up. "My Dad's the pastor of Concord Baptist Church near here and I guess I could pray with you in the morning."

"Awesome," said Ian. "I'll meet you here before class."

When Blue heard the boy mention the Concord Baptist Church, he said, "I think we're going to be in that church in a couple weeks."

The pastor's son said, "Yes you are. My Dad said you were coming."

"Great," said Ian. "I'll bring a bunch of my friends to hear you."

"So, we left it at that," recalls Blue, "and I didn't see or hear from Ian until we spoke at Concord Baptist Church two weeks later."

An unorthodox start

In the meantime, Ian began doing exactly what Blue told him to do. "Talk to God," Blue had said. "Tell him exactly what is on your heart. Ask Him to work in the hearts of your friends so that they will also turn their lives over to Jesus."

The next morning, as Blue was told later, the pastor's son, met with Ian in front of the school. Ian started talking to God just like he would have talked to any of his acquaintances.

"God you know [he named a kid who had been giving him trouble] and how that blankety-blank has pulled all that stuff on me. You know what the blankety-blank did. Well..." After a minute or two of that kind of language, the pastor's son, who couldn't handle it any longer, walked away. When Ian had finished praying he stood there with his head bowed, expecting the pastor's son to pray, but nothing happened. He looked up and realized that he was all alone, so, he just went on to school.

The next Wednesday Ian showed up at Concord Baptist Church. The pastor, who had been told by his son about Ian's "prayer language," asked him to meet him in his office.

"My son told me that you started to cuss when you were talking to God," said the pastor.

"Well sir, Iris and Blue told me about Jesus and I got saved. Blue told me that if I had friends I wanted to get saved I was to tell God about them. I told God about [he named someone] and how he blankety-blanked me."

"Whoa, Ian. God doesn't want you to use that kind of language. You can't talk like that anymore. You're going to have to clean up your speech."

"They never told me that. I just said what I thought. Blue said I was to tell God what was on my heart."

"Well," said the pastor, "you are. But now you are a different person; you've turned your life over to Jesus and there are things in your life that He wants to change. One of them is some of the language you have used. My son is willing to meet with you to pray before school starts tomorrow morning, but remember that God doesn't want you to use filthy language when you talk to Him."

Ian began working on his vocabulary as the boys met to pray on Thursday and Friday morning. They continued to meet on Monday, Tuesday, and Wednesday of the next week. That was the Wednesday Blue and Iris were to give their testimonies at Concord Baptist Church, and Ian was excited about seeing Blue and Iris again because he had not only been working on his vocabulary, but he and the pastor's son had been witnessing to some of Ian's schoolmates.

As Blue and Iris stood to speak, out in the congregation sat Ian and six of his friends. As the invitation was extended, down the aisle came Ian, leading his friends to the altar. They were all saved that night! After the service Ian and the pastor's son told Iris and Blue that every morning they had been praying for each of their friends by name.

"What an impressive illustration," recalls Blue, "of how God can use a young lad, barely saved, to shake up a school and church through prayer, witnessing and trusting God to use him to lead others to Jesus."

Their last Aussie "G'bye"
It was now nearing the time for Blue and Iris' final farewell to their Aussie brothers and sisters with whom they had bonded so closely during this ministry trip to the land down under. It is never easy to say goodbye to anyone you love, but for Christians "goodbyes" are never truly final, as there is always the anticipation of another reunion, either in this life or the next.

When the day arrived, since their flight did not leave until 9:30 that evening, they spent the better part of the day saying their farewells and celebrating Iris' birthday, which just happened to coincide with their departure.

The Nixes, along with several pastors, gathered at the *Hyde Park Plaza Hotel Penthouse Suite* to celebrate. The Hyde Park management had been so touched by the ministry of Blue and Iris that they had upgraded them to the *Penthouse Suite* at no extra charge for the several months they were in Australia.

The day before, Blue had gone to *David Jones,* one of the fanciest stores in the southern hemisphere, to have them bake a birthday cake with iris flowers sculptured in the icing. To this, he added a bouquet of 50 beautiful iris flowers. He did not plan, however, on the gift of a large bottle of champagne provided by the Hyde Park management. It ended up being put behind the door since this party didn't need any of that kind of "spirit" to help them celebrate.

An airport surprise

Birthday party over, they headed for the airport. When they arrived, Blue and Iris could not believe what they saw. Standing there to greet them were Ian and 12 of his friends. Though the kids were sorry to see the Blues leave, they were excited that Iris was now carrying a miracle child in her womb that had been conceived in Australia, in spite of every doctor having told her that she could never have a baby due to all the abortions she had gone through. They were thrilled to have been among the first Blue and Iris had told. Now, there they all were, smiling from ear to ear, waving and holding up a banner that read:

LOVE YOU BLUES—G'DAY AND G'BYE[22]

---

[22] The banner remains one of their special keepsakes.

103

"It was an emotional time," recalls Blue. "There were lots of tears when they rolled up the banner and gave it to us."

"We hope our prayer group will keep growing and that a lot more kids will get saved," said the pastor's son.

"Is there anything special you want us to pray about?" asked Ian.

Blue: "Ian, we need you to pray for Iris because a doctor has told us that she may not be able to carry the baby to full term. Pray for the baby. As for me, I would like to find my family. I don't know where my brother is or if he's even alive. Pray that I'll be able to find Bruce Blue. Remember that name—Bruce Blue.[23]"

"Goodbye friends…"
"G'bye Blues…"

Answered prayer

God heard the prayers of Ian, his friends, and others who shared Blue's concern for Iris' safe delivery of the baby and for his desire to somehow connect with his brother, Bruce. The answer to both would intersect almost nine months later in a most unusual way.

---

[23] Answer to prayer: Applewood Baptist in Aurora, Colorado

16

A "Lei"²⁴over in Hawaii

As difficult as it was to say g'bye to their "down-under friends," Blue and Iris could not help but anticipate the layover they'd be making in Hawaii to visit their friends, Colonel Dan Buttolph and his wife, Shay, whom they had not seen in several years. Colonel Dan and Shay, who had been instrumental in opening up many of the NATO base schools in Europe to the Blues' ministry, were now stationed in Hawaii.

A dateline surprise

When Blue and Iris landed in Honolulu they were not ready for the surprise that awaited them. Having crossed the International Date Line, it was still May 30, Iris' birthday. This had not been lost on the Buttolphs, although they did not let Blue and Iris in on what was in store until that evening when Dan and Shay took them to a beautiful restaurant located inside an aquarium.

Their table was located right next to the aquarium glass where you felt you could reach out and grab the fish swimming by. While they were eating, and watching the fish, suddenly a diver swam up to their table, holding a sign that read:

HAPPY BIRTHDAY IRIS

---

²⁴ A garland, traditionally Hawaiian, usually made of flowers and hung around the neck.

105

He then stuck the greeting to the window and swam off. This was just one more expression of God's love and another special memory to carry with them for the rest of their lives.

And that wasn't all

After months of intense ministry in Australia, these few days of R&R were most welcome. Among the many new experiences was getting to dine in the exclusive *Officer's Club* in Pearl, which was typically reserved for the rank of full bird colonels and up. Dan Buttolph delighted in bringing high-ranking officers to the table to meet them, which was his way of expressing his conviction that being in the Lord's army was of greater worth than that of this world's military.

At one point Blue and Iris were even cleared to attend a *Pacific Fleet Briefing* where the location of every US Navy ship in the Pacific theater appeared on a large wall-to-wall screen, along with the object of each mission. Getting clearance to participate in this briefing was a miracle because Iris's ex-con status was supposed to prohibit her from that type of military security clearance.

More fun

The fun was just beginning. Colonel Dan provided them with what he called his "clunker" *MG Midget* to drive around the island. Because of their size, the seats had to be pushed back almost to the rear bumper, and with their heads sticking up above the windshield, wind blowing in their faces, they took off.

Everywhere they went, they were treated with the utmost courtesy and favor as soon as the Colonel's MG, which was well known on the island, was recognized. Lady Iris and Sir Blue felt like royalty, which indeed they were—**Children of the King of kings!**

Unexpected Lagniappes

Surprises such as these are sometimes hard to put into words—those extra blessings the Lord brings into our lives. There is a French-Cajun word, however, that comes close to describing what we're talking about. Folk in southern Louisiana would call what Blue and Iris were experiencing, God's "lagniappe" (pron. lahn-yap). Lagniappe can be defined as that unexpected surprise, that little something extra like the cherry sitting on top of the whipped cream that is on top of the ice cream—that special something added to what is already wonderful.

Though God has surprised Blue and Iris with many *lagniappes* over the years, the most special was the one Iris was carrying "in her incubator," as Ian and his friends described it; the surprise the doctors had told Iris never to expect due to her past lifestyle. But God, knowing the heart desires of His two children, overruled what was supposedly medically impossible, and now, whereas two Blues had gone to Australia, three Blues were heading back home to America! *Denim Allen Blue* would, in approximately six months, be joining his Mom and Dad, as two became three.

Section Four

Pressing On

"Brethren, I do not count myself to have apprehended, but one thing I do, forgetting those things which are behind and reaching forward to those things which are ahead, I press toward the goal for the prize of the upward call of God in Christ Jesus."[25]

---

[25] Philippians 3:13-14 (NKJV)

17

Big Boy, Big Changes

As the time approached for their baby's birth, Blue and Iris were faced with a dilemma—their only car was a VW bug that had no back seat. They had had to remove the seat in order to push the front ones all the way back to the trunk in order to accommodate their size. Since the Texas law required that a child be placed in a child's seat in the rear, they were going to need another vehicle.

Several weeks before Denim's birth, Blue and Iris had been in Tennessee with Bro. Manley. He preached on faith, and as he often did, he asked them what they were trusting God for. Blue told Manley that they were going to need another car by the time the baby was born. So they were trusting the Lord to meet that need. Blue also told him that he was asking God to find his brother Bruce, if he was still alive.

Prayer answer number one: Bruce Blue

When they returned home they received a surprise phone call. It came as a result of detective work a lady in Applewood Baptist Church in the Denver, Colorado, area had done in response to Blue's asking the church to pray that he somehow might find his brother. She had told him that she knew ways to track people down, and if his brother was still alive, she felt he could be found. Unknown to Blue, his brother was actually living in Colorado.

God was at work to fulfill Blue's desire and to answer the prayers of Ian and his Aussie friends. Two weeks later the telephone rang.

"Hello. This is Bruce Blue. Am I your brother?"

Laughing, Blue said: "If you are Bruce Blue you must be my brother. Where are you?"

"I live in the Denver, Colorado, area. A lady got in touch with me and gave me your number."

"Well, if you can come, I want to fly you to Dallas. I'd like you to be here when my baby is born."

Prayer answer number two: A car

Bruce was sitting with Blue and Iris in their home in Seagoville, Texas, when the knock came—the knock with the second answer to prayer.

"Hi. My name is Chip Reynolds. I'm a member of Exciting Eastwood Baptist Church in Tulsa, Oklahoma. My wife, Janie, and I gave this Mercury station wagon that is sitting in your drive to the church three weeks ago. Ruffin Snow, our pastor, told me to drive it down here and give it to you. I've got a ticket to fly home in about an hour. Will you drive me to the airport in 'your' station wagon?"

Blue's brother, Bruce, witnessing this miraculous provision of a car, joined Blue and Rick for the drive to the airport. On the way, Rick turned to Bruce, sitting in the back seat:

"What do you think about your brother and his wife? What do you think about the way they live and the way they talk about Jesus? Have you thought about what you're going to do with Jesus?"

At that point Bruce did not yet know how miraculous the gift of the car was. He did not know that only Bro. Manley, and God, knew about the need.

Prayer answer number three: Denim Blue

What else to call a boy whose last name is Blue? It took very little imagination to decide on what they were going to name their son.

111

Denim arrived at 9:45 AM on November 30, 1987, weighing in at 10 pounds. But it was not only into the Blue family that Denim was born; he was immediately "adopted" into the family of *Robinwood Baptist Church*. It was here that he and his parents would be surrounded by the love and care of an extended family made up of eternal relatives.

And then there were the Beasleys who would unofficially adopt Denim as their grandson. In fact, Bro. Manley arrived at the hospital soon after Denim was born. When he was told that only family members were allowed in the room to see Iris and her baby, he posed as Denim's grandfather, a role he actually played over the years. Bro. Manley was one of the first to see and to hold Denim.

My Son

"I'll never forget the day we drove to the HEB hospital for the birth of a baby we were never supposed to have. Dr. Turner, who delivered Denim, said: 'This is going to be a big baby.' I thought, 'You don't have to go to college to know that with both parents being over 6 feet tall and weighing more than 300 pounds, that the baby would be big.'"

They let Blue witness the birth, but they had to put two gowns on him because a single one was not large enough to go around him. Then they couldn't find coverings for his shoes that were large enough, so they decided to use what Blue called, "hats" (the head coverings worn by attending physicians). There he stood, all 350 pounds, wrapped in two hospital gowns with "hats" on his feet!

Blue cried and praised God through the whole process. When Denim was finally delivered by C-section, the doctor handed him to Blue and said, "Take him and leave the room. We have to do an emergency procedure on your wife. Her blood pressure has gone dangerously low. I've got to try to save her life."

Waiting outside were Jim Everidge, Robinwood's pastor, members of the church, Manley Beasley, and Bruce Blue.

Looking back

"It was an incredible experience watching him come into the world, screaming," recalls Blue. "Denim was the first baby I had ever held in my arms. I just stood there, praising the Lord. Every year, November 30 is Miracle Day on our calendar. Miracle Day and Father's Day are very special to us. It blows my mind to think how much I love my son, and how much my Heavenly Father loves me.

"After Denim was born, I remember reading these words in Proverbs: 'Listen my son...Listen my son...'. I read them over and over. In the past I had always felt that God was speaking to me as a Father, but now I began to see that I had the awesome privilege of speaking to my own son. I realized that the Creator of all life had given me something that I in no way deserved; not just eternal life, but a wonderful wife and an incredible son."

Never the same again

With Denim's arrival things would never be the same again. The child they had dreamed about was now a reality, and with him came major adjustments at home and on the road. Denim would begin his formal education at *The Pathway to Learning School* where he'd continue until Mom and Dad decided that he needed to travel with them full time in their ministry. This meant he would have to be home-schooled.

Home schooling? No problem. With the help of materials available in print and on video, Iris could do that. And while they were at it, why not add Blue as a student since he was still working on his own reading and writing? And perhaps, if all went well, both Blue and Denim could matriculate together. They did!

Travel—the best education

With all the challenges of learning "on the go," there were also advantages, such as experiencing first hand many of the things written in their history and geography lessons. This kind of learning turned out to be easier for father and son, as both of them are dyslectic.

You want to know about the Holy Land?[26] Ask the Blues. At this writing, Iris has been there 23 times, Blue, 13 times, and Denim has been to the land of the Bible every year but two since he was nine years old.

On one of these trips Blue and Iris discovered that Denim had a beautiful voice and was born with a fine musical ear. One day, as the Blues were leaving a pizzeria in Jerusalem, Iris spotted an ice cream stand across the street. She immediately broke into song: "Thank you Jesus," to which Denim spontaneously echoed, "Thank you Jesus." Every line she sang, he repeated, and before they knew it they were harmonizing.

And so Denim entered the "music ministry." It would not be long before he'd be joining his parents in song and eventually singing solos in their meetings. Singing and sharing his own testimony have become a very important part of Denim's life and calling. Then, in 2007, he began to address an important issue in today's church life, especially in the "western" world.

What is salvation?

"When I was seven years old one of my school teachers in *The Pathway to Learning School* at First Baptist, Seagoville, told the class about how Jesus had come to die for our sins and that if we believed in Him He would take our sins away. I said: 'I want to do that.' The teacher said, 'Well, Denim, if you really want to know the Lord, ask me tomorrow.'

"She was a godly lady and she didn't want us kids to make a quick decision without having time to think about it. She wanted to test and see if we understood what it really meant to be saved.

---

26 For information regarding future Holy Land tours led by the Blues see contact page at end of book.

"The next day, when I told her that I still wanted to meet Jesus, she said, 'OK, ask me tomorrow.' After about four days of this, she finally said: 'Alright, Denim. Let's go into the hall and we'll talk about it.'

"I prayed what she told me to pray, though at that time I really didn't understand what I was doing. The best way I can explain it is that I thought that if I gave God my heart He would give me a home in heaven. It was kind of like a tradeoff. And that's how I thought I would live the rest of my life.

"I soon began travelling around the world with my parents, and though I was basically a good boy, I always felt that there was something missing, especially from the age of 16 on. I didn't know what it was until December 30, 2007, when Jim Everidge, our pastor at Cornerstone Baptist Church in Lucas, Texas, preached his Sunday morning message. I can't even remember what he said; all I know is that I went to the altar.

"That morning I understood for the first time that God didn't just want my heart, He wanted everything that I was. He had given His all for me and He wanted me to give my all to Him—my past, all my failures, all my successes, my future, everything. I look at that day as the day of my conversion; the day I was saved.

"When I give my testimony I tell people that I was never a scumbag like Mom and Dad were. I didn't do all the things that they did. Those who knew me would say that I was a good boy, but I'm here to tell you that it took as much of the blood of Jesus and grace of God to save me, a good boy, as it did to save my scumbag parents."

18

A Tale of Two Cakes

Where presented? Churches large and small, including First Baptist, Dallas, TX; school assemblies, universities, conferences and camps; prisons; the War College in Carlyle, PA; NATO school assemblies in Europe.
How? Two tables on which two mixing bowls and the cake-baking ingredients are placed.
Why? To visually demonstrate the life-damaging results of a rebellious heart.

Blue: "Here are two mixing bowls and the ingredients for two cakes. Now, before we get started, I want to know how many of you will volunteer to eat the cake I'm about to bake, or how many want to volunteer to eat Iris' cake?"

(Without fail, every time this is done, about 99% volunteer to eat Iris' cake. There are always a few, however, who dare to choose Blue's "offering.")

Blue: "OK, that's fine—but don't be deceived, God is not mocked. Just remember that whatever you put in the bowl comes out of the oven. Whatever you plant, you harvest." (Blue's free translation of Galatians 6:7)

Blue then starts to read the directions on the back of his cake-mix box. "Prepare cake mix as indicated on box. In large bowl..."
Iris interrupts: "You stupid or something. You don't know how to bake a cake? You have to read the directions? I don't need to follow what's on a box. I know how to bake a cake. I don't need to be told what I'm to put in it."

"Excuse me, lady. I don't mean to be rude. I'm just trying to do what it says. 'Combine first three ingredients...'"

Iris interrupts him as she opens a pack of cigarettes. "Here, smoke some of these." She takes them out, breaks them up, drops them in the bowl, and dumps a box of cake-mix on top of them.

Then she opens up a can of chewing tobacco and says: "Here, if you don't want to smoke, chew. Put it in your back pocket. I always say: 'If you don't want it on your lip, put it on your hip.' You'll look so cool, pulling it out of your hip pocket and sticking a wad in your cheek."

Blue: "My instructions say: 'Add three eggs, one at a time, beating well after each one.'" Blue then picks up three eggs, but before he can crack them open Iris grabs them and throws all three into her bowl, shells and all. She starts smashing them on top of the cigarettes and chewing tobacco.

Iris: "I can tell that you think I'm being rebellious in what I'm doing. Well, I can tell you that my cake is going to be better than yours when we're through because my ingredients are my choice. My cake is going to be made up of what I want, not somebody else's ideas."

Blue: "My directions say add oil." When Blue begins to measure out the cooking oil, Iris takes a quart of motor oil and begins pouring it into her bowl. While Blue keeps measuring everything he's putting in his bowl, Iris measures nothing. She just dumps one thing after the other into her cake mix.

Blue: "Mine says, 'Add baking soda.'" He measures it out and adds it to his bowl while Iris pulls out a bag of marijuana (they use parsley that doubles for marijuana) and throws it in the bowl. By the time Blue says his directions say add some water, Iris has pulled out a beer bottle and pours the contents into her mix (the bottle actually contains ginger ale).

She then says: "Look, yours just lays there. My cake foams."

Blue continues: "My directions say, 'Mix thoroughly.'"

At that point Iris turns on him. "Look punk. You don't smoke, you don't chew, you don't do drugs, you don't drink, you don't... Nobody's gonna like you. You don't have any rebellion in your life. There's nothing exciting. You're just a drag."

Then, as she throws jalapeño peppers into her bowl she says: "You know, you should have sex out of marriage. Why not? That's hot stuff!"

When they finish mixing their ingredients, they pour what they have onto two separate cookie sheets and Blue puts them in an oven. (Cookie sheets make it possible to bake their concoctions in about 15 minutes.) As he goes to the oven, Iris begins telling her story.

"Do you think that I planned to go to prison when I was young? Nobody does..." After sharing for about eight minutes, Blue takes the balance of the time to give a brief account of his story. He begins by saying:

"Everyone puts ingredients into their lives. But what you may not realize now is that the ingredients you put into your life doesn't only affect you, it affects others. The ingredients I put into my life during my early years contributed to my mother's suicide. Your life is always going to affect others. My ingredients caused my mother's death. I didn't put the pills in her mouth that killed her, but the choices I made, the ingredients I put into my life, caused her to take over 200 pills that day. I never hurt her physically, but what I did with my life, my rebellion, my anger, my demands, my insisting on doing things my way, ruined her 'cake' and destroyed her. What we often forget is that every choice we make affects others around us."

After briefly sharing his story, Iris returns with both cakes. They are covered with chocolate frosting and look so smooth and pretty. Nobody in the building can tell them apart. Blue then asks: "Who wants to eat Iris' cake now?"

Blue continues: "There are always one or two brave hearts, especially in schools and camps, who want to show how macho they are. We always invite them to come forward. The others, 99% of them, change their minds. We call that 'repentance'. They have repented of what they had initially chosen.

"The ones who don't repent, however, the ones who refuse to change their minds, are the best illustration of all, because the human stomach cannot tolerate motor oil. It's physically impossible. It will come out. It won't hurt you, we've checked it out with doctors, but it definitely is going to come back up. Once they eat a piece of Iris' cake it won't be more than 10 seconds before they go running down the aisle."

Blue and Iris recall how, at a summer youth camp, a handsome jock, a young man all the girls had their eye on, said he was going to eat Iris' cake. Once he had committed himself he wasn't about to back down, so up he came. He looked and acted so cool with his shirt unbuttoned.

"When he took the first fork-full," Iris laughs, "you could see a cigarette butt sticking up. But that wasn't about to bother that 17-year old. He chomped down on that piece of cake, butt and all, chewed it up and swallowed it. Nothing was going to stop him."

"Wow, this ain't going to bother this fellow," Blue thought, as he reached for the cake. "Hey, get yourself another bite." They watched him, kind of defiantly, take the second bite. As he did, they could see everything in him begin to change. The first bite had hit bottom! The color left his face and the next thing you see is him heading for the 50-gallon trash barrel that was standing nearby. He barely made it…W-a-a-jquash! The girls couldn't believe what they were seeing.

As he was bent over, Iris said: "How many of you want to kiss him right now?"

After things had settled down, and many of the young people had made their way to the altar, having been confronted with a spirit of rebellion or other spiritual needs in their lives, Blue thanked the young man for being such a good sport. Later on in the day, when they saw him again, Blue jokingly asked him if he would be willing to travel with them as their designated "pewker." They laughed, but it was a lesson that young man would never forget.

Summary

The Tale of Two Cakes has a sobering message for us all. It boils down to each of us checking on the ingredients we are daily adding to the "cake" of our own life. Do the ingredients we choose demonstrate a spirit of rebellion toward God as we focus on what we want to do or have, insisting on doing things our way, or, are we following the *Manual of Instructions* that God has provided for us? Think on these things!

A Tribute

What Duane Blue Means to Me

Charlie Minney—Southern Baptist Associational Missionary,
Coalfields Association, West Virginia

There have been very few people who have impacted my life for Jesus like Duane Blue. A lot of folks know the Blue who will pull out his bag of tricks and have the entire crowd wondering how in the world he did that. Many know the Blue who will challenge every guy's manhood with a simple balloon, which I still can't blow up. They may know the Blue who stands Empire State Building-tall and is as big as the state of Texas, but not many people take the opportunity to get to know the Blue who has a heart bigger than Alaska, the Blue who truly loves the "least of these," or the Blue who desires everyone to know the Jesus who so deeply loves them.

As I try to put what Blue means to me into words, I think of a *Man of Conviction,* because Blue showed me that we must have convictions based on God's Word in order to stand tall in a world of people who are going against everything we believe in.

Then again, he could be described as a *Man of Faith.* I have seen VERY FEW in my life who are living out the faith life that Blue lives in order to impact the world. I'm talking about simply trusting God that He is who He says He is, that He will do what He says He will do, and that He is a God who truly does desire what's best for us.

You could also describe Blue as a *Mentor.* When I was a custodian at First Baptist Church, Woodstock, Georgia, Blue would intentionally set aside one day every week to show me, and several others, how to study God's Word and how to apply it to our lives. He even gave most of us our first Greek-Hebrew word study Bible. It is partly because of his mentoring that my family and I are serving on the mission field today with the North American Mission Board.

121

Considering all the words I've used to describe parts of the Blue I know, there is one word I believe that best describes my good friend Blue. It is a word that sets him apart from many today. It is the word, *real.* In a society where so many people are writing, speaking, and singing what they believe people want to hear, Blue is sharing what they <u>need</u> to hear. In a day when so many in the church have gotten away from sharing the hard truths of God's Word, when many have gotten away from standing on the promises of God, when many have gotten away from truly proclaiming the Word of God, Blue keeps clinging to those things with all his being. He represents God well!

You can rest assured, whether it is in a restaurant, in a grocery checkout line, a small rural country church, or in a mega church, when Duane Blue stands to speak, he will "give 'em heaven!"

I pray that as you read through this book that God will bless you, change you, and help you get to know the man I'm honored to be able to call my friend—Duane Blue.

19

Roll That Stone Away!

"Jesus said: 'Remove the stone...' So they removed the stone..."
(John 11:39, 41, NASB)

Blue: "His dead body had been wrapped in burial clothes and placed in the family tomb. He'd been in there four days when Jesus finally arrived. There was no way that Lazarus would ever again see the light of day. You could beg him, you could con him, you could tempt him with a million dollars, but there ain't no way Lazarus was ever gonna come out of that tomb, unless...

"When Jesus told the people who had gathered to remove the stone, *he was telling them to do the only thing they could do,* as Bro. Manley used to say. Since they couldn't tell Lazarus to come out of the tomb, the only thing they were capable of doing was to remove the stone. And when Jesus told them to do that, they said: 'No way. He's been dead four days and he stinks by now.' Even Mary and Martha didn't believe that there was any hope for their brother. At least they were denying that there was. So how could rolling the gravestone away do any good? Let's think about that. Let's see how this can be applied to us.

The denial stone
"The stone in our lives can be anything that we deny. For eight years Iris' mother denied that her daughter was in prison. She denied that Iris was lost. She persuaded herself that Iris was just backslidden so that if Iris did die she could stand over her coffin and say, 'Oh well, now she is with Jesus.' It was for her own comfort that Mirrell Urrey hid the truth. And when she

realized that, she had to move the stone from her life, which was her living in denial over her daughter being in prison.

"Iris' mother is one of the best illustrations I know for what it means to remove a stone that keeps a loved one from Jesus. When she finally confessed to her Sunday School class, to her pastor, and to the whole church that she had been lying to them about her daughter, two weeks later, as you can read in the story of Iris' life, her daughter knelt down a tramp, on the sidewalk in front of one of her topless bars, and minutes later she stood up a lady, transformed by the blood of Jesus.[27] And God used a young man to witness to her who had no idea what her mother had finally done. He had no idea that God had been waiting on Mirrell Urrey to remove the stone from her own life before He would turn her daughter's life around.

"That stone can be all kinds of stuff. It can be lust, greed, anger, anything that keeps us from hearing and doing what God wants us to do. When I share this message I tell people that there may be something in their lives, a stone, a stumbling block that is keeping other folk from hearing God's voice and from being everything they can be in Christ. What if there is a stone in my life that keeps someone in my family, or a friend, or someone I work with from hearing Jesus' voice? I don't want to have to answer to that. I'd rather go to my son, Denim, 10 times a day to tell him I'm sorry rather than to be a stone that keeps him from Jesus."

Sitting in the audience one night, when Blue was talking about the stone, were Randy and Jan, the parents of Zack who had met Blue at the Vacation Bible School where he had turned into a robot from outer space. Zack had invited Blue to go home with him for lunch and it was not long before Blue became a part of their family.

Zack had made a profession of faith not too long after that, but as he got older he showed little evidence that he had

---

[27] See, *IRIS: Trophy of Grace,* for full story

experienced a genuine conversion. His parents, however, had held onto his profession as a child and were praying that he would rededicate his life and get right again with God.

When they heard Blue talk about rolling the stones away from our lives they realized that their stone was similar to Iris' mother's stone. They were living in denial that Zack was lost. They came, broken to the altar, saying that all those years they had been praying for Zack to rededicate his life. Now they were going to pray for his salvation. Blue had explained that God doesn't answer a prayer that can't be answered. When you pray for someone to rededicate their life when they have never received Christ as Savior in the first place, it's not a prayer God can answer. They also soon learned that the prayer for a "lost" child is more desperate than a prayer for a child to just "get right." You can't "get right" when you're dead.

The short-fuse stone

An itinerate minister also came to the altar that night. He was broken. He said, "I've been in the ministry for years and I need to get right with my son. When I'm on the road I'm gracious to other people, but when I go home I can be mean and sharp to my son and the other children. I see this as a stone that can keep them from hearing Jesus speak—from becoming all God wants them to be. I need to roll that stone away."

The embarrassment stone

The pastor and his wife listened carefully as Blue told how for years Iris' mother had lived in denial and embarrassment that her daughter was in prison, and how it wasn't until she got honest with herself, the Lord, and her church, that Iris was saved. When the altar call was given, the pastor and his wife responded. They had an *embarrassment stone* that needed to be rolled away. They had not been able to tell their congregation that they had a son serving a life sentence in prison.

A Testimony

Larry Rice, *Hope for Hurting Hearts* Ministry

I first heard Iris give her testimony at the 1980 Texas Baptist Evangelism Conference. At the time I had no idea what a divine appointment that meeting would prove to be for me and my family in the years to come. After serving as youth pastor at First Baptist Church, Sherman, Texas, I was called as senior pastor of Emmanuel Baptist in Pittsburg, Texas. I asked Iris to share her testimony at Emmanuel, then after she and Duane were married, we had both speak numerous times over the years.

I have always appreciated how authentic Duane is in his witness for the Lord. He pulls no punches and tells it like it is for the glory of God. When Duane got saved he really "got it," and is continually sharing the story of God's miraculous makeover in his life.

In the spring of 1990, Blue and Iris were scheduled to be with us again. This was at a pivotal point in my life as a pastor. Our son, Andy, had been arrested for a serious crime, committed while under the influence of drugs. We had walked with him through his trial and now, the week before Blue and Iris arrived, Andy had been given a life sentence to be served in the *Estelle Unit* in Huntsville, Texas. Since all of this had been taking place in another part of the state, the church did not know anything about it, and due to the embarrassment it was to us, we had not been able to tell the church what we had been going through.

When Duane and Iris arrived I told them that, because we had not told the church that we had a son in prison, I was going to resign as pastor at the end of the Sunday morning service. My faith was being tested as it had never been before, and I knew that if anyone could understand what our family was going through it would be Blue and Iris. They prayed with us, encouraged us, and said, "Let's just see what God is going to do."

When I looked at the Sunday morning crowd, many of them visitors, and saw the incredible response there was to Blue's sermon, I began negotiating with God. I told the Lord that I was still going to resign, but maybe it would be better to wait until the evening service when the crowd would be smaller and there would be fewer visitors.

Well, it seems as though sometimes God has a sense of humor. That night the crowd was the largest we had ever seen and we had to bring in extra chairs. The Lord used Duane and Iris to again bless the hearts of our people, and as Duane preached his message, *Roll the Stone Away,* God gave me peace in my own heart, peace that He would be with us in the midst of the storm we were going through. My wife, Linda, and I went to the altar and as the service was closing I told the church that we needed to have a "family time" because I had something important to share with them.

When mainly our church members remained, I told them about our son Andy. I told them that since the crime and trial had happened out of town, most, if not all, did not know what we had been going through. I told them that since we had not been open with them in letting them know that we had a son in prison, I felt that I no longer was worthy to be their pastor and that I was now tending them my resignation. As I began to read the letter I had written the night before, the chairman of the deacons stood to his feet and called out, "No pastor. We will not allow you to resign. You will be an even better pastor now than you've ever been before because you will better understand our heartaches and hurts."

As he was speaking, it seemed as though the whole church rose to its feet. Our people surrounded Linda and me, many of them weeping, praying for us and expressing their love for us. God used the Blues that day to set the tone for the response of our people. I will never forget that night as our church family committed themselves to begin praying for Andy, that God would break through the stubborn rebellion in his life.

It had been hard for me to believe Blue when he said that Andy's going to prison was the best thing that could happen to him. I struggled with that, but I lived to see what Blue said come true. Eight years into his sentence, Andy slipped into the back of the prison chapel on a Wednesday night and told God that he was sick and tired of being sick and tired and that he wanted God to change his life—but if God didn't do that, he didn't want to live any longer. That night our son surrendered his life to the Lord Jesus and made a complete 180-degree turn. He started to regularly attend chapel and eventually would become the chaplain's assistant.

Andy began attending faith-based programs, enrolled in college by extension, and began seriously studying the Bible with his cellmate who had also become a Christian after his incarceration. For the next 10 years Andy lived a life sold out to Jesus, winning many of his fellow inmates to Christ. They saw the difference in Andy's life and they knew that if God could do it for him, there was hope for them. They observed that *Bulldog* (Andy's nickname) had more than religion, but that he had a relationship with Jesus Christ.

Over the years Blue and Iris prayed with us that Andy would remain a strong witness behind the "walls." God heard our prayer. Through a miraculous set of circumstances that only God could have orchestrated, on December 6, 2006, 18 years into his life sentence, our son was released. He was released from the bars of prison, even as he had been released from the chains of sin! Andy immediately joined Linda and me in our ministry, *Hope for Hurting Hearts*,[28] and now God is using him mightily in prisons, in churches, or wherever doors open to share what God has done.

---

[28] Hope for Hurting Hearts Ministry, Inc., P.O. Box 1245, Pittsburg, Texas, 75686. Website: www.hopeforhurtinghearts.org

This past September, *Hope for Hurting Hearts* was invited to lead a prison crusade at Huntsville's *Estelle Unit,* the very prison where Andy was incarcerated. The Warden wanted a "success story" of someone who had been in that prison and who had made it in the free world. The chaplain told the Warden about Andy and our ministry. We invited Duane, Iris, and Denim to join us for that weekend, along with several other team members. That weekend over 70 men stepped forward to pray to receive Christ.

The Lord had brought the Blues and the Rices full circle after 32 years!! As we look back, we see how God brought Blue and Iris into our lives at a moment when we were facing one of our most difficult periods. They would not let me forget that Romans 8:28 is true. I am one who will be forever grateful for the touch of God on my life through Duane and Iris.

Roll that Stone Away!

Concluding his message, Blue reminds us that when the folk at Mary and Martha's place finally do roll the stone away, Lazarus, lying there dead, wrapped in grave clothes, heard Jesus' voice — **"Lazarus, come forth."** At that moment the Spirit of God responded to the voice of Jesus, and raised Lazarus from the dead.

Blue asks: "What is the stone in your life that is keeping people from being able to hear Jesus' voice? What's keeping you from rolling your stone away so people can hear Him cry out, **'Come forth...'"**

20

Breaking the Curse

Death row

Warden*:* "Do you have a final word you'd like to say?"
No. 999441: "Yes sir. First of all, I want to say that for many years I did things **my way** which caused a lot of pain to me, my family and many others. Today I have come to realize that for peace and happiness you have to do things **God's way.**[29] I want to thank my family for their support. I love you. I also want to thank the chaplains I have met over the years who brought me a long way. I also cherish you as my family. And at this time…oh, Ken, my little son, I am coming to see you. Oh Lord, into your hands I commit my spirit. Thy will be done."

Warden: "Do you have a final word you'd like to say?"
No. 999485: "Yes, sir. I am going to start with the victim's family. I know I took someone very precious to you. Please forgive me. God has given me peace. I love each and every one of you. This was the only way God could save me; I would pay it back a thousand times to bring back your loved ones. I would pay it gladly. Mom, you didn't do anything wrong. Thank you, Warden, thank you Chaplain, thank you God, I am ready to go. God please take me home. I'm ready Warden. Thank you Jesus. I'm going now, mom."[30]

---

[29] See end of chapter for *My Way—God's way*

[30] These "final words" are but a few of those on record. Some refused to say anything, while others' statements were bitter. Many, however, were a testimony to the effective witness of chaplains, Christian wardens, and

When Blue, Iris, and Denim visited the *Estelle Unit, Huntsville, Texas, State Maximum Security Prison* in September 2010, it housed just over 3,000 inmates. In *Collfield*, another unit that houses just under 5,000, 319 were on Death Row, 10 of them women. Though the Blues had ministered many times in prisons and jails over the years, this was one of the few times that they had taken their son, Denim, with them, and he was a bit anxious as he heard one barred gate after another clang shut behind him.

God, what do you want us to say to these men?

As the Blues listened to several speakers from the ministry team they were with, they began thinking of two verses in Deuteronomy 5:9-10: "...I, the Lord your God, am a jealous God, visiting the iniquity of the fathers upon the children to the third and fourth generations of those who hate Me, but showing mercy to thousands, to those who love Me and keep My commandments."

Though neither Iris or Blue had ever considered using these verses in a prison setting, they suddenly realized how applicable these verses were for those inmates who had gathered to hear them, and especially in light of their son, Denim, being there.

"Jesus became the curse for us," Iris thought. "And He broke that curse when he rose from the dead, so, when we receive Jesus and He becomes our life, the curse is broken. It doesn't have to go to the third and fourth generations like the Scripture says."

There's hope!

When it was the Blues turn to speak, Iris said: "I know that no matter what you are, Christian, Muslim, Hindu, Buddhist, or just nothin', late at night after you've been locked down and you are lying in your bunk with just your thoughts, you hope

---

others in prison and jail ministries who are responding to Christ's words in Matthew 25:36, *"I was in prison and you came to me."*

that nobody of your family is going to end up where you are, especially your children. You sure don't want them to follow in your path. Though you may not believe in God, you still hope there is someone who will protect them from messing up their lives like you have. You pray, 'Don't let 'em come here. Whatever they do, don't let 'em end up here.

"But you know, and we know, that the odds are they will, because just like some of you they will follow in the steps of family members: brothers and sisters, parents, uncles and aunts. You were influenced by them, and for some of you, this doesn't just go back to them, it goes back to your grandparents and their generation. Now you wonder if you are going to end up passing it on to your kids and grandkids.

"It's kind of like you're living under a curse and you're wondering if there is any way to break it. Well, me and Blue," continued Iris, "have brought you a gift tonight. We've brought proof that the curse can stop right here, with you. We have brought you evidence that a curse can be broken."

Pointing to Denim: "When our son, Denim, was born, he could have had two strikes against him. His parents had really messed up their lives by every sin you can think of. His parents spent time in jail and prison and if something had not happened to them, if something had not happened to us, and changed our lives, and if something had not happened to Denim, he would have followed in our old footsteps.

"There are verses in the Bible that talk about this. They talk about a curse being passed down to the third and fourth generation of families who hate God. But we're here today to tell you that it doesn't have to be like that. The curse that the Bible says goes on to the third and fourth generation of those who hate God can be broken by just one generation that turns to Him for help. That's the generation the Bible says God will love. When you meet Jesus and give up on going *your way* and choose to go *His way,* the curse can be broken."

When the men heard those words, they all jumped to their feet, applauding and shouting. They had just heard that there was hope. They heard that life didn't have to keep going on like it had. They were hearing that there was a way of getting off the out-of-control carousel they found themselves spinning on. They were hearing that there was a way of escape from the hopeless cycle that was destroying their lives and would destroy the lives of loved ones. At that point, Denim got up.

"I wasn't a scumbag like my parents were, but it took just as much of the blood of Jesus to save me that it took to save them. I could have had a double curse on me because both of my parents had really messed up, but when they broke the curse in their lives, their influence led to the curse being broken in my life when I repented of my own sin and gave my life to Jesus."

He then sang a song, a cappella, that talked about needing to find answers when your circumstances leave you in "fear and despair" and that the answer can only be found when you "come to Jesus."

When Denim finished, they all stood again, cheering as though they had caught the meaning and spirit of the message Denim had shared. Some of them wanted to reach out and touch him.

Double jeopardy or grace?

What grace! Blue had no Christian influence whatsoever from either side of his family. His dad, Russell Blue, was married eight times and ruined the life of every single one of his wives. Blue's mother was the first one, and after almost destroying her, he took off, leaving her with two little boys.

Then on the other side of the family, his mother committed suicide at age 40, and statistics show that children of parents who commit suicide are twice as likely to commit suicide themselves.

As for Iris, her parents were churchgoers, and though she had been brought up going to church from nursery age, in her preteen years she got into drugs and ran away from home at 13. It was not until 15 years later, after multiple arrests, eight consecutive years in prison, and many abortions that she considers murder, that the curse was broken.[31]

Take two lives with their kind of history, getting together and having a child, what hope could there be for their offspring, other than the curse being broken, both in the parents' lives and in the life of the child? Only Jesus!

My way or God's way?

Frank Sinatra and Elvis Presley recorded a song that had the recurring phrase, "I did it my way." Doing it "my way" is exactly why millions are imprisoned, not only behind physical bars, but in their own personal prisons, choosing to turn their backs on God by insisting to seek the answer to life in going *their way*. This was what death row inmate No. 999441 talked about in his final statement: "I want to say that for many years I did things **my way** which caused a lot of pain to me, my family and many others. Today I have come to realize that for peace and happiness you have to do things **God's way.**"

The following words might well describe those of us who have turned from going "our way" to going "**God's way.**"

God's Way[32]

As I turn back the pages of my life they're so confusing,
for I confess for years I went the way of my own choosing.
I planned each hour I lived, each step I made along life's highway,
and every day I kept on going my way.

Regrets were more than few, so much I'd do met with resistance.
A life I thought was full turned out to be a mere existence.
I had no guiding light, I'd seldom seen a bright or clear day,
and every day I kept on going my way.

---

31 Read her story in *IRIS: Trophy of Grace.*
32 Words by Ron Owens. This poem may be sung, but not recorded, to the *My Way* music or to an original music setting by Ken Medema.

For what is man, what has he got,
if just himself, then he has not
but broken dreams and emptiness,
a life of fear and loneliness,
yet every day, I still would say,
"I'll do it my way."

Then:

One day I saw the hopelessness of life I had been living,
and tried to cover up the memories of a life of sinning.
While hurting deep inside my heart longed for a new, a right way,
that's when I heard a voice say, *"Why not God's way?"*
Then He revealed His Son who died for me on Calvary's mountain,
and from that wounded side there flowed a tide, a cleansing fountain
that washed away my sin and turned my night into a bright day,
and in my heart I knew that this was God's way.

But:

They buried my Lord, and thought they'd won,
for He was dead, but they were wrong!
The angels rolled that stone away
and from the tomb He rose that day,
fulfilling what the Scriptures say,
"He did it God's way!"

And:

He's coming again, this risen Christ,
who gave Himself in sacrifice,
and every tongue shall speak that name,
and every nation loud proclaim
to Him who shall forever reign,
"JESUS IS GOD'S WAY!"

21

Who are the Blues?

Trees, Jewelry, a Gourmet Kitchen, and Nonstop Scripture

A visit to the Blue home, no matter the time of year, is an unforgettable experience. None, however, is quite as special as the Yuletide season.

A Christmas Tree Forest—Indoors!

So you decorate one Christmas tree each year? How would you like to decorate 34 distinctly different ones? Thirty-four is actually the largest number of trees Blue and Iris have had in their home during the Yuletide season.

Each of these trees has a particular story behind them. Some represent countries where the Blues have ministered, some are reminders of special events in their lives, and some interpret various aspects of the Christmas story. Here is a description of less than half of what you may find on any given Christmas visit.

The Jesus tree: Everything about the birth of the Savior.

The Australian tree: Kangaroos and koalas with many other memories of their four ministry trips to the land down under.

The German tree: Greens and reds with gifts received and items purchased from their extensive ministry over the years in Deutschland.

The kitchen tree: Located in the kitchen with various cooking items.

The fruit tree: All kinds of different fruit that Iris says represent various expressions of the *Fruit of the Spirit.*

The crown tree: *Crown Him with many crowns!* All sizes from those small enough to put on your finger, to large enough to wear on your head.

The Czech tree: This could be called the "blue and white tree" as it is decorated with beautiful blue and white china from Czechoslovakia.

The gold tree: Covered with gold decorations and reminders of one of the precious gifts the magi offered to the Lord Jesus.

The crystal tree: Crystal from all over Europe.

The angel tree: Angels collected from "everywhere."

The necklace tree: Necklaces from all over the world, including Blue's own jewelry creations.

The Denim tree: Could also be called the "toy tree." At this writing, it has seen 23 Christmases in a row and is covered with toys, teddy bears, and gifts that Denim has received from all over the world.

The Holy Land tree: Beautiful olive wood creations, items dating back thousands of years, including a vase that was made 700 years before the birth of Christ and items that tell the story of both Old and New Testament days.

The singing tree: Three feet tall, placed in the guest bathroom. Beware! This tree is motion activated. As you walk in, its eyes and mouth open as it begins serenading you with Christmas carols. The singing tree has spooked many an unsuspecting visitor!

Jewelry

The Apostle Paul made tents—Blue creates witnessing jewelry.

In 1986, when Blue began travelling more with Iris, it meant he was not able to work as much in construction as he had initially planned. As this was to be his part in helping support her ministry, he began asking God to show him what he might now do, as they both were of the conviction that they were not to send out appeal letters.

The idea of making "witnessing jewelry" originated at Kirby Woods Baptist Church in Memphis, Tennessee, where one of their ladies gave Iris a witnessing bracelet. She showed Iris how to us it, and that evening, after church, several of the women went to Taco Bell where Iris used the bracelet to lead a young lady to Jesus.

When Iris returned home she asked Blue to call the lady from Kirby Woods who made the bracelets to see how they might acquire 10 more, since Iris had given the one she had to the young lady in Taco Bell. The bracelets arrived, and within two weeks those 10 were gone. Blue, seeing where this was heading, called the lady "bracelet-maker" to see if she would consider telling him how he could make the bracelets himself.

"Are you good with handling small objects?" she asked.

"No ma'am," he said. "I have great big hands and have never worked with small things."

She said, "I'll send you the material for 10 bracelets and you see what you can do."

What she didn't tell Blue was that he was going to need tools, and that without them it was going to take hours to make just one. It did!

Finally, however, after he had finished those 10, she told him the kind of equipment he would need to make multiple bracelets in the time it was taking him to finish one. She offered to sell him some used tools, real cheap, as well as a video that explained how to do it. Blue was on his way.

Some time later, his aunt, who also made jewelry, heard what he was doing and gave him some rock-cutters. With these, along with the widow's mites and ancient coins he had begun to buy in Israel, he now had everything needed to produce not just witnessing bracelets but also other beautiful Christian jewelry—jewelry with a message.[33]

A Gourmet Kitchen

Hobo dinner, anyone?

Blue cooked over an open fire for years. He invented a dish that, if he had marketed it, would have made him a bundle of money because what he invented was later promoted by Reynolds Aluminum. Blue called his creation a *Hobo Dinner.*

"I'd take ham, hamburger, or chicken, and I'd slice up carrots, potatoes, actually almost anything you want to put in it, then I'd wrap it three times in aluminum foil and just throw it in a fire. Forty minutes later when I pulled it out, it was cooked. Reynolds aluminum promoted this on a TV commercial for their tin foil. They demonstrated how to cut up the contents and how to fold the foil so as not to lose the juices. It was just like I used to do," recalls Blue.

He points out that you can also put it on the engine block of your car and in about 200 miles down the road you have a cooked meal—if it hasn't fallen off.

Blue barbequed chicken every single weekend for years. Wherever he was camped, he would serve from five to 50 people. It was so tasty people would ask what his secret was, and he came up with a line for what made his barbeque so special.

"I use only black honey that comes from Black African bees," he'd tell them. It of course was a lie. All he did was take any kind of honey and mix 4-5 tablespoons of vanilla in it and it would turn black. Vanilla, of course, was one of the ingredients

---

[33] See Appendix One for additional witnessing jewelry information

he needed to add to the hickory barbeque sauce that he would put on the chicken. He had all his biker buddy friends and campground neighbors believing him for years.

One of Blue's specialties over the years was chicken wings. He'd cook up to 200 wings at a time for his biker buddies. "I'd wire them together and hang them over an open fire. I even did this in Walmart parking lots," recalls Blue.

Little did he realize that his skill and love of cooking would one day be linked to Iris' gift and interest in the culinary art, and that this would become one of their special ministries wherever they lived.

A Woodstock Christmas

Wherever they have their church membership, Blue and Iris put together an annual Christmas food-fest for their church staff. This includes an invitation to everyone from the pastor to the secretaries to the custodian and all their spouses. None, however, was, or ever will equal, the size of their first Christmas meal for the staff of First Baptist, Woodstock, Georgia. Nor has any been put together as quickly as was that Christmas feast.

Up until this year it had been quite manageable, with the largest staff numbering only 17. Now, however, they were dealing with a church that had a membership of many thousands, and a staff with spouses of more than 180.

How, when and where?

They were faced with more than the challenge of numbers. They had only arrived in Woodstock on Thanksgiving weekend, which left them with just a couple weeks to get ready. No sooner was their furniture in place than they began preparing for the big event. With a bit of detective work and gentle persuasion, they found people and places that would give them discounts and even occasionally contribute to the cause.

Now, all they had to do was figure out how to accommodate that large a number in a 1,500 square-foot house. No problem.

They had a basement! They would divide the staff and their spouses into groups, each group assigned with a specific time to appear, over a three-day period.

In a gourmet kitchen everything is made from scratch. Blue was up each morning at 3 o'clock preparing his own special recipe of seafood gumbo made with shrimp, chicken, sausage, rice, and a few other "secret ingredients." For those who did not like gumbo, Iris was making her own special vegetable and beef soup, using only the finest tenderloin. Then, added to these was what they called their "lack-nothing" salad bar, topped off by an 8-foot dessert table. But that was not all. As the guests left, they picked up their own special gift—something for the ladies and something for the men.

This went on for the six years Blue and Iris lived in Georgia, and this expression of love and appreciation would become one of the highlights of the season for the staff. And so it was, and so it will continue to be wherever they are, as long as God gives them the strength.

Nonstop Scripture
"Faith cometh by hearing and hearing by the Word of God."

In the background of any visit to the Blue's home you will hear the nonstop reading of Scripture. It is subtle, but it is there. At any moment, wherever in the house you may be, living room, kitchen, bedroom, or bathroom, you can pause to listen to Alexander Scourby reading God's Word.

It has been Blue and Iris' conviction that since *"faith comes by hearing and hearing by the Word of God,"* they would have Scripture read in their home around the clock.

Through the years verses have jumped through the speakers at strategic moments with a word applicable for a particular need or question.

22

Woodstock Tributes

*The following tributes are by several of the Blues'
close friends from their First Baptist Church,
Woodstock, Georgia, days.*

Phillip Byrd, staff member

It is a privilege and huge honor to share how Blue has impacted my life. The first time I ever saw him and Ms. Iris, they were sharing their testimony at our church, First Baptist, Woodstock, Georgia. I hadn't been saved very long, and boy, could I ever relate to what Blue was talking about because I had a similar background in drugs and I hadn't been off them all that long when I heard his story. I knew then that he was someone I needed to meet someday.

At the time I had no idea the Lord had much bigger plans, and that actually, Blue and I would eventually become great friends. I consider him to be one of my closest friends on earth. He has taught me so much and has invested so much of his life in me as he has helped me learn more and more about the Lord Jesus.

Just like Blue, when I got saved I couldn't read either, so he gave me the Bible on cassette, just like Ms. Iris had given him. This helped me learn to read as I listened and followed along in the Bible. We started a Bible study in his home every week, when he was in town. There were five or six of us who made it most weeks. Blue gave me a Greek-Hebrew Bible and commentary to study with. He told me that this would help me to "scuba-dive" into the Word, to get down deep.

This helped me learn that I could turn to the Lord every time something came my way by opening God's Word. I also found out that fellowshipping with other Christians helps get you through tough times, too. I experienced this in a profound way when one of my daughters was killed in a car accident. Blue will never know, this side of heaven, how much he helped me as well as many others.

My very first mission trip was with Blue. He and Ms. Iris helped do a camp for underprivileged children in Texas and I got to be a part of it. I left there more blessed than anyone. This was a big step for me. I had never really been out of town very much and to put myself out there to talk to strangers was very stretching, but I grew through it, and it ended up being one of the best things that could have happened to me. On that trip I learned that I could love others and it was OK to let them love me back.

Over the years I was able to attend other events where Blue was speaking. This always blessed me. At one of these events God showed me something big that I needed to do and Blue helped me with it. I hadn't always been good to my wife over the years and something Blue said at a men's conference showed me that I needed to renew my vows to her. When I got saved she had said that finally she had the husband she'd always dreamed about. Now I knew that I needed to show her just how much I really loved her. I decided to have a renewing of vows ceremony. Blue and Iris helped me plan the entire thing and we kept it secret from my wife until the day it happened. Blue officiated, and it was one of the biggest blessings our marriage has ever had.

Blue and Iris have played a huge role in our lives. They have taught us to rely on God for everything. Blue taught me that I should pray with and for my wife and family every day. Everything I have learned about how to have a better relationship with the Lord and with my family I learned from Blue. There is a saying that "the only Bible people in the world may read are your actions." I thank the Lord every day for a friend who is obedient and different who makes me want to have what he has—to be like him.

I praise the Lord for Duane Blue and the eternal investment he has made in me. I praise the Lord for a friend who is always there when I need him. I praise the Lord for the blessing he has been to me and my family. The Blues are family to us and we'll be forever grateful (Philippians 1:3-6 & Proverbs 27:17).

Traci Byrd, staff member

My husband, Phillip, and I first met Blue and Iris through some mutual friends, and I tell you, we haven't been the same since! To say they are a blessing to EVERYONE they meet is an understatement! They are true-blue friends for sure, who love you unconditionally! They have blessed us beyond words.

We used to go over to the Blues' house (when they were in town) at least twice a week. We always had the best time. There would be a lot of great food, good times, game playing, Scripture reading, ministering, and prayer! They would always challenge and stretch us in a good way. We learned that, *since the fruit is not on the tree trunk, you have to get out onto the limb to experience the fruit, and sometimes that is scary, but always well worth it.* There were always six to 10 of us there at a time. For about four years we spent almost every holiday with them.

My husband, Phillip, has shared what a great impact Blue had on his life. I sure can testify to that. He was a drug addict for years before the Lord delivered him from that addiction and not long after that, He brought the Blues into our lives. This happened at a point when Phillip really needed a friend like Blue, a friend who could understand him, help him, pray for him, challenge him, and hold him accountable. And Blue was all that, and more, to my husband. Let me tell you about one very special way God used Blue to bless us.

Years ago, when Phillip was not doing well, one of many hurtful things he did was to sell my wedding rings so he could buy drugs. I was devastated, and I never had a real ring from then on. When Phillip began studying the Bible with Blue, he confessed some of the things that he had done, and especially what had happened to my rings. This triggered an idea in Blue's heart. He suggested to Phillip that it would be really neat for us to renew our vows. So, the planning began, without my knowing anything about it!

Blue helped Phillip get a really nice set of rings for me that I wear to this day! And since this was to be a surprise for me, Blue and Iris led me to believe that they were having important guests coming in from Texas and that they needed me to help entertain them. So I began decorating their house.

Blue already had a beautiful pulpit in the living room and Iris had him build an arch over it, which we decorated. In the meantime, several of our friends, who had been in on the plan, were also helping out.

It was not out of the ordinary for the Blues to give gifts such as clothes, jewelry, etc., so I was not suspicious when they bought my friend and me new dresses to wear to serve the guests. And they had the guys wear tuxes.

The day came for the event, and as I was hurrying about to get ready, Iris called and asked me to go by the bakery to pick up some petit fours. This meant that I would be the last to arrive, which was all part of their plan. When I walked in and discovered that the big party was for Phillip and me to renew our vows, I was overwhelmed.

My family and friends were there. Blue performed the ceremony with words that our pastor, Johnny Hunt, had written for him. It was a magical time. It was not only a very special time but they had fooled me all week into decorating for my own wedding and picking up my own wedding cake—sneaky, sneaky, but awesome.

You would not believe the people they involved in this. I have never been surprised or treated so special in my whole life. They also arranged for us to stay in a hotel that night, and Iris had gone that day to put the BIGGEST flower arrangement and basket of goodies in the room for us. When we arrived, the hotel staff knew right where to send us because they remembered the beautiful flowers that had been put in our room. For someone who is a "behind-the-scenes" kind of person, something like this was huge to me. I later told Iris that I felt like the Lord had finally given me the husband I had always wanted, and that they had played an enormous part in this.

I have learned tremendously from Blue and Iris. I have learned from their example! I am a better person for knowing them!

Linda Holland, staff member

The Blues have the gift of hospitality. They know what it means to love on people and they do it with everything they have. From the time they moved to Woodstock and joined First Baptist Church, every year, without fail, they had the entire staff over to their house for a Christmas luncheon. They served 180 of us with a smorgasbord that would knock your eyes out. Blue would spend days peeling shrimp for us while Iris was baking pies, treats and side dishes that would make your mouth water.

They had to schedule it over a three-day period in order to work us all in. One year we knew they were hurting financially because of Iris being sick, but they wouldn't let the church pay for any of the food, so we as a staff just hid money all over the house in Christmas trees. Now, that's another story. Christmas trees! We would go over right after Thanksgiving and help them decorate the trees! There were trees everywhere, and every tree was unique.

They made the staff feel so loved, special, and cared for. I truly believe every staff member really looked forward to the Blues' Christmas luncheon.

As a part of what we called the "clique" I used to spend some great hours with Blue and Iris at their house, just talking about God's Word and playing games. I miss those times. It was a very sad day when they moved away!!

Virginia Stephen

As a part of the "clique" I also helped decorate the Christmas trees and assisted with those great Christmas staff luncheons that the Blues put on every year. But as memorable as those Christmas times were, even greater memories for me, and something I'll never forget, were the intimate visits with them.

The Blues have an incredible way of teaching one to live by faith. When my husband became ill and was no longer able to work, they quickly reminded me that this didn't take God by surprise. They started to challenge me to trust Him to meet our needs. With that, my husband and I took God at His Word and began the journey of faith, trusting in His provision. And the Blues walked by our side in that journey. It was exciting to report to them all God was doing to provide for us. They are the only ones who have ever challenged me to live by total faith and it has forever marked my life.

Epilogue

The Journey Continues

This epilogue begins with a tribute from the Blues' "new" pastor, Erick Graham. Providentially, God has led Blue, Iris, and Denim to the Athens, Texas, area after spending the prior five years in Lucas, Texas, where they were members of Cornerstone Baptist Church.

A Tribute
Erick Graham—pastor, Sand Springs Baptist Church,
Athens, Texas

It hasn't been that long since I met Duane and Iris Blue, but as soon as I did, we started a friendship that I believe will last a lifetime. This gentle giant of a man has a way of loving and caring for people that I believe reflects the Savior he loves so much. Blue is one who genuinely enjoys his service for the Lord. He never bought into the lie of cheap grace and man-centered salvation, but has been joyfully giving of himself, his time, and his resources ever since the moment Christ purchased him from Satan's slave market. Blue has already given me more than I can ever repay, and I am not alone.

Soon after I met Iris and Blue, they invited a group from our church to visit them in their home. After Iris had spoiled us with her great cooking and loving hospitality, Blue invited the guys to his converted garage where he spends much of his time. As he shared with us about how he studies God's Word and how every man ought to treat his wife, I wondered how many had received these same life-lessons before us. We left completely inspired, as the overflow of the 'God-filled' Blue family splashed over onto us. Everywhere they go, they seem to be splashing on those around them, and I do mean everywhere.

It doesn't matter what the setting is, Blue is going to share the gospel with someone. Using balloon animals, slight-of-hand tricks, or his best robot voice, Duane genuinely loves sharing the good news of Jesus Christ. In fact, genuine is one of the best words that I can think of to describe him.

From faith to faith

To know the Blues is to know three individuals totally devoted to each other and totally committed to serving their Master, whatever the cost. Transparent, sometimes to a fault, and discerning to a tee, Blue, Iris, and Denim live on a "faith plain" that, in the world of today's Christianity is hard for some to understand. They have never doubted that God could do anything, and this has led to their sometimes getting out on a limb. When this happens, you might hear them quote something that Bro. Manley once told them—"I'd rather be around a man who misses God running straight past Him, than a man who misses God standing still." They also believe that "you can have as much of God as you are willing to pay the price for."

Being thoroughly persuaded of the truth found in Hebrews 11:6 that, "without faith it is impossible to please God," they desire and seek, not to live by "common sense," but by what they have been taught about the life of faith from the early days of their Christian walk, such as Manley Beasley's well known definition:

> *Faith is believing something is so, when it is not so, in order for it to be so, because God says it is so.*

Though some may say that Blue and Iris *march to a heavenly drumbeat that not many people hear,* they'll be the first to say that they are far from having arrived in the walk of faith.

"I'm sorry," says Blue, "but I've made a lot of mistakes. I see so little faith in my own life. True faith is one of the hardest things to get a hold of. I'm very glad though, that the Lord brought Bro. Manley into my life early on. He taught Iris and me about faith as much by the way he lived, as by what he said. For the first eight years of our marriage, whenever we had a problem or question, he was always there to help us find our way. I don't think he ever told us what to do, that wasn't how he operated, but he would help us look into the Scriptures to find the answer.

"We were in Israel when he died. We flew straight back to Dallas, Texas, in time for the funeral at First Baptist Church, Euless. I was asked to be a pallbearer. It was the first time I ever did anything like that. We really miss him.

"We keep looking for the kind of faith that is taught in the Bible, but we don't see a lot of it in today's churches. Though there are exceptions, so many seem to be operating the way the world does. They base their budgets on what they think their members are going to be able to do, not on what God may want them to trust Him for."

And so the journey for Blue continues. Those who are watching him will observe that he longs to be God's man, showing the reality of the presence of Jesus through his life, whether in the marketplace, with other believers, or in his home. There is great reason to believe that Blue will finish well because his confidence is not in his own ability, but in the faithfulness and power of the One who called him out of darkness into HIS glorious light. And we do have this promise that:

"He who began a good work in (Blue) will perfect it until the day of Christ Jesus" (Philippians 1:6, NASB).

Appendix One

Additional Tributes

The following tribute is by Blue's sister-in-law, Evelyn Urrey-Dendy, better known by family and close friends as Punkin. Part of her story is found in the biography, IRIS: Trophy of Grace.

When Ron asked me to write a tribute about Blue I was at a loss for words. I wasn't sure if I could adequately express my thoughts about someone else, especially a family member, without sounding either too complimentary or too critical.

To start with, Blue came to our family one Christmas as someone our family could reach out to and love. He was a big, hairy dude, who lived alone in a bus with two dogs. He had been working with my brother, Ernest, who invited him to join us for Christmas as one of my sister Iris' weirdoes. You could tell he wasn't used to being around family gatherings. My sister, who was a *Mission Service Corps volunteer* with the *Home Mission Board* of the *Southern Baptist Convention,* and my brother began to share Jesus with him. I wasn't sure if Blue was really receiving it or just conning them.

Months later, after he was saved, I was absolutely shocked when my sister Iris told me she was dating Blue. It was difficult for me to accept this because at that point all I could see was who he was and not who he could be. Then, when she told me that they were going to get married, I really had to pray for God's peace. I was still looking at Blue with a critical eye, but I was beginning to learn that God always has a plan, and I was starting to learn that His ways are not our ways—or in this case *my ways*.

Through the years I have watched as God, through his precious refiner's fire, has taken that old man Blue, and made him into a new person. And as God did this, he placed in him the desire to be a strong witness for the Lord. When I think of Blue and his methodology, I think of Elijah or John the Baptist, who the Bible describes were both rough-shod men—men who lived in the wilderness, alone. I can imagine Blue like that. They were not weak or timid men, but were men who loudly proclaimed God's word with boldness, just like Blue does.

There have been times when I would question God—Lord what are you thinking?—and He always ever-so-sweetly reminds me of who I used to be, and what He has done in my own life.

I recall one time when I was visiting Iris and Blue at their home in Georgia, how Blue had invited a man over who was a member of their church but who had stopped attending and had fallen away from the Lord. Blue shared the word of God with him and cried out to the Lord in prayer. He showed this man a genuine concern about his relationship with Christ. As a result, this man was restored and had his life turned around.

Blue has the ability to reach people for Christ who seem unreachable by others. He has made this his life's goal. Along with my sister, Iris, they have won more people to the Lord than I can even imagine, proving that God can take that which man deems worthless and He can make it priceless. I thank the Lord for the awesome work he has done in Blue's life, and what he has accomplished in taking this strong man, with all of his weaknesses, and using him for His glory. And it ain't over yet!

A Tribute

David O. Cofield—pastor, CrossRoads Baptist Church
Rogersville, Alabama

The woman at the well (John 4) had an immediate impact on her hearers when she went back into the city. I believe the reason she had an impact is because they could easily compare the person she had been to the new person they were seeing.

There was a sense of her just being real, and that can be said of Duane and Iris Blue. While we may not have known them prior to their conversions, it almost seems as though we did, when we hear their testimonies that grip our souls. And definitely we have witnessed how "real" they are as they speak "the truth in love," witnessing to the power of the gospel of Jesus Christ.

Of all the times I've been privileged to have with Duane and Iris, the occasion I will remember the most is when we arranged for them to be a part of the Colbert-Lauderdale Baptist Association in Alabama for 30 days in March 2008. They spoke in over 25 churches, plus schools and jails. Churches of all sizes got to hear the powerful testimonies of this awesome couple. And what a difference it made. One pastor, who had them for three days, said, "It was the best three days the church has ever experienced."

When you think of the Blues, they have many stories that make you laugh or cry. One of my favorites is how Blue, when asked how much it would take to get Iris to come to a church to speak, replied, "God saved her from charging for her services. That's what she did in her previous life."

Duane and Iris, we love you and thank God for you. You are real. Keep loving Jesus, loving people, and sharing the love of Jesus with whomever will hear.

Appendix Two

The Witnessing Bracelet

Dark Crystal = **Sin**
　　"All have sinned..." (Romans 3:23). *"The penalty of sin is death..."* (Romans 6:23).

Red Crystal = **The Blood of Jesus**
　　Jesus paid sin's debt with his own blood (Romans 5:8).

Clear Crystal = **Forgiveness and Purity**
　　The blood of Jesus cleanses completely through and through (1 John 2:12).

Blue Crystal = **Waters of Baptism**
　　A picture of your salvation & obedience (Matthew 28:19).

Green Crystal = **Growing in Christ**
　　Study God's Word and pray (11 Peter 3:18).

Gold CrystaL = **Streets of Gold**
　　Revelation 21:21—*"And the street of the city was made of pure gold, like transparent glass"* (Revelation 21:21). One day, all born-again believers, either by death or rapture, will go to heaven where the streets are made of gold!

Purple Crystal = **KING OF KINGS**
　　"He (Jesus) has written on His robe, and on His thigh: KING OF KINGS AND LORD OF LORDS" (Revelation 19:16). One day, we all will bow at the royal feet of the Lord Jesus, and worship Him.

PHOTO
GALLERY

Blue's 6th grade picture, the last year he attended school and the year he began smoking tobacco and marijuana. No photos have been found between age 13 and the picture taken below when he was living in his Berserko Bus in Tomball, Texas.

The converted school bus and his 3-wheel motor trike

A "berserk" pose inside the bus

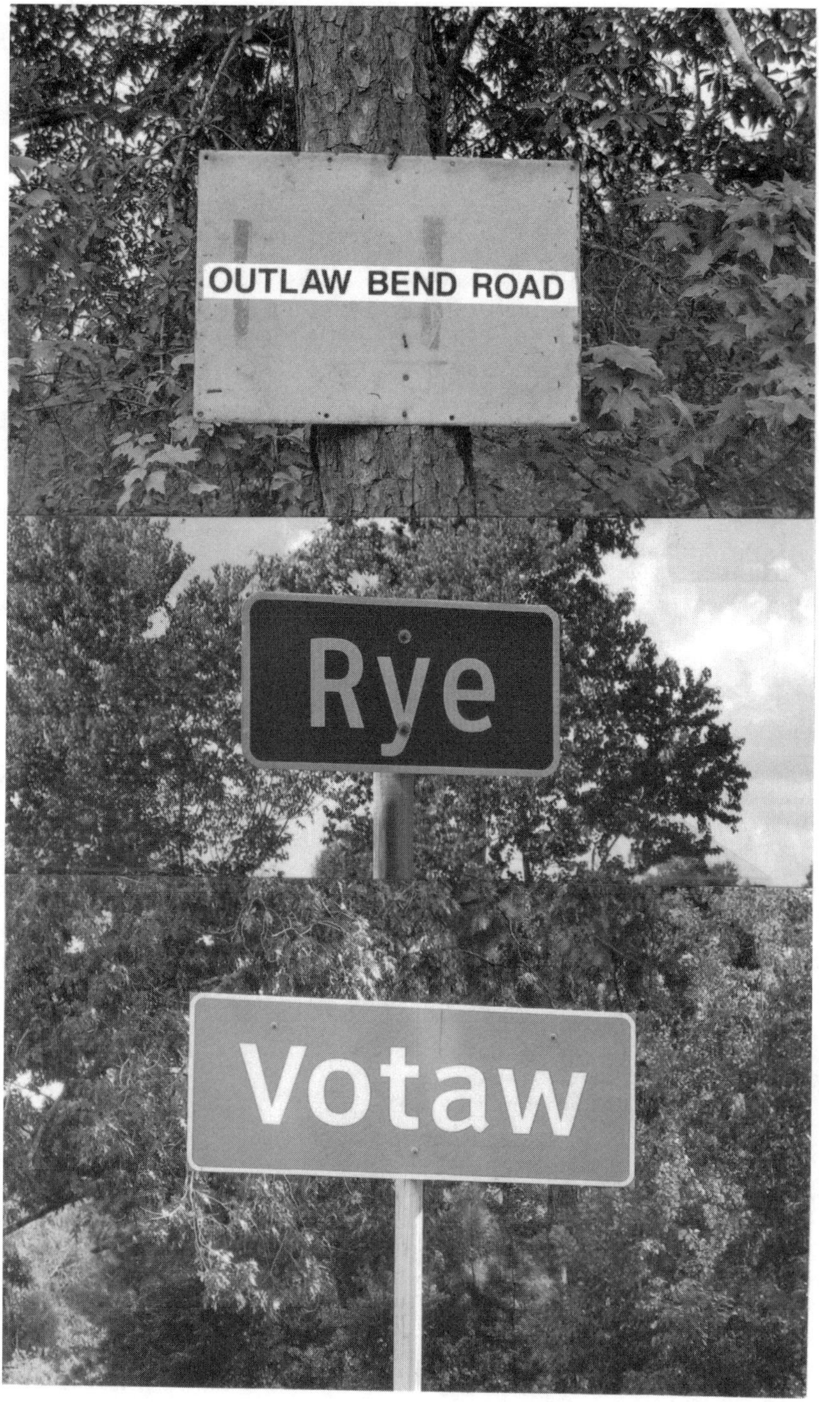
OUTLAW BEND ROAD
Rye
Votaw

The December 9, 1984 wedding at First Baptist, Votaw, Texas

Vlado and Ruth Fajfr in their Zilina, Slovakia, home

Driving Dr. W. A. Criswell around at Texas summer camp

Iris and Blue in their VW "bug" soon before Denim was born

Australian Outback hat and Aussie paraphernalia

Blue on his Harley. See knife collection in background.

The Nativity tree with the Denim (toy) tree on the right

Blue in his workshop, creating witnessing jewelry

One of the many Holy Land tour groups the Blues have led

Blue teaching on broken cisterns that cannot hold water, at En Gedi, where David hid from King Saul

"Balloon ministry" with Israeli soldiers at St. Stephen's Gate, Jerusalem, where Stephen is thought to have been martyred

The Blue family: Duane, Iris and Denim

General Information

To order copies of *Call Me Blue,* visit

www.ronowensbooks.com
www.duaneandirisblue.com
www.hannibalbooks.com
or
other online and physical bookstores

Additional Contact Information

Duane Blue
Email: dblue7777@yahoo.com
Phone: 770-845-4101
www.duaneandirisblue.com

Ron Owens
Email: ronowens3@gmail.com
Phone: 479-366-1341
www.owensministries.org

Other books by Ron Owens
Return to Worship
Worship: Believers Experiencing God
(co-authored with Henry Blackaby)
They Could Not Stop the Music
Manley Beasley: Man of Faith, Instrument of Revival
IRIS: Trophy of Grace
The Milldale Story